WHEN REVELATION COMES

JIM HARTSELL

Foreword by Michael Bamberger
Afterword by Wright Thompson

Back Nine Press
Chicago, Illinois
www.back9press.com
Twitter and Instagram: @backninepress

9 8 7 6 5 4 3 2 1

Second Edition
Printed in the United States of America.
Book design by Asya Blue

Library of Congress Cataloging-in-Publication Data:
Hartsell, Jim.
When Revelation Comes : A Journey Across the Sacred Links of Scotland /
By (Author), Jim Hartsell, Back Nine Press (USA)
pages cm
ISBN 9781956237092 (hardback)
ISBN 9781956237054 (e-book)
1. Non-Fiction. 2. Golf. 3. Golf courses—Scotland 4. Grief and loss.

*This book is dedicated to my father Lee Hartsell,
and my sons Jonathan and Jake.*

They loved Jordan as much as I did.

TABLE OF CONTENTS

FOREWORD

BY MICHAEL BAMBERGER

This is how I met him: this most extraordinary man, father, golfer, architect, artist, and writer.

A package arrived at the kitchen door, announcing itself. I picked it up.

The delivery man waved over his shoulder and returned to his tall brown truck.

I considered this newest arrival.

It's an everyday thing, these days. Home delivery of this, home delivery of that. We've all become used to it.

In my house, most of the packages are for Christine, but this one was for me.

What is it?

Whatever it was, it's protected by a firm cardboard shell with a red *pull-here* tab. I pulled as instructed, with the hint of anticipation running through me. Out came a hard good, spine first but not breached. By habit, I opened the book to its dedication page.

In my life, I'd never read one like it.

Below it was a photograph, perfect in its framing and composition, both arresting and gorgeous.

The author's first 18 words, the black-and-white photo from his personal archive: it's a stop-time, one-two punch so powerful it left me frozen at the kitchen counter, the open book under my chin.

I knew, on instinct alone, that I'd never fully understand the inherent mystery of this dedication page. Try as I might.

Inserted into the book, lodged almost into its binding, was a notecard. On one side there was a gentle watercolor, a landscape depicting a swath of golf course in pale colors. A stream, a bridge, a clubhouse, the hint of a mountain behind it. On the other side the author had written a note, personal in nature, in casual handwriting that wasn't cursive, but not quite print. The top of the notecard bears a memorable stamp:

Jim Hartsell
Hartselle, Alabama

This was Jim's first book, about the building of Sweetens Cove Golf Club: a remote, nine-hole, stand-alone, privately owned public golf course. *The Secret Home of Golf.* Courtesy of the back flap of the dust jacket, I read that Jim was an architect by day who worked on projects at different Southern universities, but writing about golf, and seaside golf in Scotland, were his "true passions."

I devoured the book. I devoured his magazine pieces. I drove to Sweetens Cove. Later, I got to his Scottish golfing home, Dunaverty, and played there.

Now I, like you, have Jim's new book in front of me. *When Revelation Comes.* What Jim knows about golf and life, and life and loss, is more than any parent should ever have to know. But millions do. Jim has the heart and the insight and the experience to help us see the light we might otherwise not see. This book continues where the dedication of his first book left off.

—Michael Bamberger

PROLOGUE
SCOTLAND THE BRAVE

*"Peter Alliss was on his feet in the BBC booth,
electricity surging through his old bones. 'He struck
that shot beautifully and whilst it was in the air,
I thought to myself, 'Dammit, he has done it!'"*
— Jim Huber, *Four Days in July*

It was Sunday of the 2009 Open Championship, on an unmercifully hot and humid day in Alabama. I was in my office at home, pretending to work while watching every shot being struck on the legendary links of Turnberry. The temperate climate of the Ayrshire coast would have been a welcome relief to the burning summer of the southeastern United States. It had been a few years since I had been able to visit my favorite country, but I had gotten up every morning at 2 am to watch all four rounds of the Open, not allowing myself to believe what was unfolding in the championship. I was missing Scotland more than ever.

In those precious and fleeting days, all three of my boys—ages 10, 16, and 18—still lived at home with us. Jonathan, the oldest, who was leaving for college soon, was in his room next to my office. Jake and Jordan were in the backyard hitting chip shots to a sand green we made with a yellow flag stuck in the middle. We had always been a golfing family. Both my grandfathers and my dad played, and I had taught the game to my boys in turn.

The tournament was winding down to the last few holes. Tom Watson, at age 59, had somehow held his game together for all four days, and stood poised to tie the legendary Harry Vardon with a sixth victory in the Open. As Watson approached the 17th tee, I made all three boys come into my office to watch the last two holes.

"You are about to see the greatest moment in the history of sports," I told them, ceremoniously.

The scene took my mind back 32 years to another Open Championship Sunday spent in my parents' den in Tarrant City, Alabama. That was the day Watson faced down Jack Nicklaus in the now mythical "Duel in the Sun" over the same links of Turnberry. My dad sat in his recliner by the fireplace, pulling for a miracle from his hero, Arnold Palmer. I was on the floor right in front of the television, living and dying with every four-foot putt from the final group. During commercials, I would go into our backyard and hit plastic golf balls to a dirt green I had made. Sometimes my dad would watch me hit.

Watching the Open Championship with my dad every year—but especially the 1977 Open—was the start of my lifelong love affair with Scottish links golf. To a 10-year-old in rural Alabama, Jack and Tom had seemed like gods as they stalked around the ethereal, yellowish-brown Ayrshire links. Watson made seemingly impossible 50-foot putts and chip-ins look routine, but Nicklaus would not go away. The pair pulled away from the rest of the field, with Tom shooting a remarkable 65-65 over the weekend to defeat Jack by a single stroke. The greatest player of all time could only manage to shoot 65-66. Even after all these years, I can still hear the cheers of the Scottish crowd when Jack made an impossible birdie from the gorse bushes on the 72nd hole. As they walked off the green, Jack put his arm around Tom. The Scottish crowd stood and cheered in joyful admiration for what they had just witnessed.

Hubert Green, the reigning US Open champion and a Birmingham native whom both my father and I had actually met, finished in 3rd place, a full 11 strokes back. The day after the tournament Green was quoted as saying, "I won the golf tournament. I don't know what game those two guys were playing." The legendary Palmer even managed his final top 10 finish in a major championship at age 47, much to the delight of my father. That weekend in front of the television with my dad, listening to the great ABC golf crew, was a seminal moment in my life.

It seemed fitting, three decades later, to be enjoying a similar moment with my boys, among them my own golf-obsessed 10-year-old, Jordan. He was wearing a Titleist cap and still holding his wedge in a gloved hand. Over the previous two years, he had totally immersed himself in the game with the passion that only a small child can.

With the four of us crammed into my small, book-filled office, Watson birdied the 71st hole to take the lead. I started to let myself believe a rare miracle was going to happen in a world often filled with disappointments. The boys were now fully into it too, having been raised on stories of my many travels to Scotland with my dad. They knew how much I loved places like the Old Course, Turnberry, Dunaverty, Machrihanish, Prestwick, and Cruden Bay. We talked about them the way I imagine other families discuss famous football stadiums. Open Championship weekend was like a holiday in our house. I always cooked a traditional full Scottish breakfast at least once during the tournament. I would also buy a few bottles of Irn Bru, the orange soft drink so beloved by Scots. It was a family tradition.

Most golfers reading this will know the sad outcome that day for the great Tom Watson. He hit a brilliant drive on the last, splitting the middle of the fairway. We were all standing in front of the television now. A perfectly struck approach shot caught the wrong side of a small downslope on the front of that famous green, where Nicklaus had been so gracious in defeat in 1977. The ball bounded crazily over the back and into a difficult spot. Almost in unison, we all screamed, "NO!"

When Watson badly missed a seven-foot putt to win his sixth

Open title, Jonathan and Jake seemed to sense that it was over. They went back to what they had been doing. Jordan stayed in my office to watch the playoff with me. Even at that young age, he knew that Stewart Cink came from a town in Alabama less than an hour away from us. Jordan and I had played together at the course in nearby Florence, where Cink had learned the game. There had been a small shrine to the successful PGA professional in the corner of the clubhouse dining room.

As Watson and Cink were preparing to start the four-hole play-off, my happy young son said confidently, "I'm going to play in the Open one day, Dad."

This was my boy: of course he was going to play in the world's greatest championship one day. Before that Open, I would take him to Dunaverty and Machrihanish to help him prepare for links golf. We would spend a day at Shiskine on the Isle of Arran. At Prestwick, I would show him where Young Tom Morris took possession of the Open Champions belt with his third consecutive win. At St. Andrews, we would eat lunch in the Dunvegan and walk down to the 18th green at the Old Course. The dream of every golf dad flashed before my eyes in that split second.

Children are innocent. They normally do not understand or hold onto disappointment in the way that adults tend to do. Jordan was eerily perceptive for his age. When Watson, now finally looking every bit of his 59 years, duck-hooked his tee shot on the third playoff hole, we both knew it was truly over.

"Dad, this isn't fair. Tom deserved to win. That shot on the last hole was perfect."

"That's just links golf. Even Watson would say the same. You'll see how it is one day," I replied to my son.

Twelve years later, in August 2021, I was back in Scotland, sitting on my favorite bench on Mount Zion, on the 11th hole of Dunaverty Golf Club near the Mull of Kintyre. This time I was traveling alone, with the incomprehensible realization that my sweet Jordan would never play in the Open, as he had so proudly and confidently promised, or journey with me to this spectacular place. The magnitude of my situation was impossible to deal with in Alabama. The only place it made sense to be was in Scotland, the country that had been my spiritual home for the past three decades.

Over the years, I had traveled to every remote corner of this wondrous kingdom and had come to love the Scottish people. I had played nearly 100 golf courses, and yet still had places I wanted to visit. When I was here, the stress of work and everyday life could be put on hold for a few weeks, or even a month. Scotland had always been the place where I was happiest.

The Scottish way of life—being much more present and connected to other people—is something I had always longed for. In this country, the wonders of nature, often displayed through golf, are celebrated and revered. The quiet dignity and empathy that Scots show in dealing with the inevitable tragedies of life was something I needed badly at that moment.

My visits to Scotland had produced some of the most blissful moments of my life. Together my father and I had lived out our dreams of playing the great links of this country. I had once spent a wonderful three weeks here with my son Jake, visiting places like Anstruther, Cullen, Carradale, and Shiskine. The sheer joy on his face, as we made new discoveries together, is something I will never forget.

I needed to see if that type of joy was still possible. I had come home to search for answers. I had come home to find a way to continue.

1

DUNAVERTY

"Golf is a game in which you are alone with
your Creator. The course may be crowded with
opponents, caddies, spectators and, in the case
of Dunaverty, my home course, also with sheep,
cattle and dive-bombing terns."

—Angus MacVicar, *Golf in My Gallowses*

"What's your plan for the afternoon, Jim?," asked Mr.
David Baxter, the proprietor of Ardell House, as I
met him walking on the gravel drive in front of his
bed and breakfast, located on the 18th fairway at the mythical links
of Machrihanish. It was a stunningly clear summer day in August
1994 on the Mull of Kintyre, in western Scotland. My father was
waiting in the clubhouse to meet me for lunch. We had already been
in the village for five days.

"Well, I've already bought a day ticket," I responded. "I think
I'm just going to play here until dark," as I gestured toward the

magnificent linksland across the B843. The Atlantic Ocean was impossibly blue, as if trying to outdo the sky. In 1994, a day ticket for Machrihanish was £18. In August, it never seems to get dark.

"Aye, you could do. This is certainly the day for it," said my friendly landlord. "Why don't you drive over to Southend and play Dunaverty? It's only £5. I think you and your dad would really enjoy it. It's a lovely wee course only a few minutes from here." We had made the pilgrimage to Machrihanish—then virtually unknown to American golfers—solely based on Michael Bamberger's classic 1993 book, *To the Linksland*. As great as Michael's book is—it had also led us to Crieff, Cruden Bay, and Royal Dornoch—it doesn't even mention Dunaverty. I was a bit reluctant to leave Machrihanish on such a nice day, but something in the way Mr. Baxter spoke made an impression on me. He wrote down directions to Dunaverty on a scrap of paper, stressing that I turn right at Stewarton, and I walked over to the Machrihanish clubhouse to meet my dad.

As I learned on that long-ago first trip to Scotland, which quickly became my favorite place on earth, the perfect meal is a bowl of soup and a ham and cheese toastie. The scotch broth in the old Machrihanish clubhouse—you served yourself out of a large pot—had a restorative power even greater than a golden dram of Springbank whisky. My dad was sitting in front of the large bay window in the wonderful bar/dining room waiting for me.

"We are going to a place called Dunaverty this afternoon," I said. My dad, who is always up for a new adventure, simply said, "Sounds good to me." We quickly grabbed our bowl of soup and I ordered both of us a sandwich at the bar.

My fascination with the links golf courses of the United Kingdom, and especially Scotland, started at a relatively young age. The first year I can clearly remember watching golf with my dad, a golf fanatic, was in 1975. I can still see him jump out of his chair when Jack Nicklaus made the 40-foot putt on the 16th at Augusta on his way to defeating Johnny Miller and Tom Weiskopf. Later that year, I have a vague memory of watching Tom Watson and Jack Newton on the last few holes at the Open Championship at Carnoustie.

The next year the Open was at Royal Birkdale, and I remember how excited my dad was with Johnny Miller's win, but we were both more fascinated by an impossibly young Seve Ballesteros, who seemed born to play links golf.

It became obvious that the Open Championship—the British Open to many Americans—was my father's favorite golf tournament, even more than the almost sacred Masters. Like many children at such an impressionable age, it also became my favorite tournament. When the Open came to the stunning Ailsa Course at Turnberry in 1977, I remember waiting for the *Birmingham News* to arrive in the afternoon so we could see the first-round and second-round scores in the sports section. Birmingham, Alabama native Hubert Green was in contention! A few weeks earlier, I had seen a few photos of the Ailsa course in *Golf Digest.* I was fascinated by the images. Turnberry looked like nothing I had ever seen before.

Then came the tape-delayed ABC broadcast on Saturday: with Jim McKay, Dave Marr, Bob Rosburg, Jack Whitaker, and the great Peter Alliss. There was usually a cold open lead-in from the host McKay—*quickly out to 12, where Jack Nicklaus has 10 feet for birdie to take a one stroke lead over Tom Watson*—or something to that effect. It was enough to send chills down your spine. That weekend we watched every shot of the greatest golf match ever played, which would later be called the Duel in the Sun. I was transfixed by the beautiful brown and green links and the way the ball seemed to roll forever. Nicklaus and Watson were like two superheroes. For whatever reason, in the mind of a 10-year-old golf fanatic from Alabama, I decided that this was the way golf was meant to be played. I became obsessed with the Open Championship venues, always on links courses by the ocean, and I could recite them the way other kids would recite the starting lineup of the Cincinnati Reds or Boston Red Sox. At some point that weekend in 1977, I remember my dad saying, "I want us to play in Scotland one day."

Seventeen years later, now a registered architect in north Alabama with two small children of my own, I found myself with my dad in a rented Vauxhall Senator on the narrow, winding road from Machrihanish to Dunaverty. We had already played Prestwick, the Old Course, Carnoustie, Cruden Bay, and Royal Dornoch on this long dreamed of trip. I had played a minimum of 36 holes a day for the previous four days at Machrihanish: one day even walking 54. *To The Linksland,* and a phone call with Michael Bamberger himself, had been my guide for planning everything.

As we entered the small village of Southend, it suddenly felt exciting to be going to a place that I knew virtually nothing about, not even from my library of golf books or numerous magazine articles on Scottish links that I had collected over the years.

Two weeks into this trip, which would turn out to be one of the seminal events of my life, I was already addicted to Scottish culture. The genuine friendliness and dry humor of the people, the wonderful food, the beauty of the countryside—especially the wild and rocky west coast of Kintyre and the islands—were things I had not anticipated being so moved by. There was a constant feeling of being in an ancient and holy place. The world was condensed and moved at a slower pace. Even with all these great things, Scottish golf—both the courses and the culture—had been the overriding revelation.

All of the famous places had more than lived up to my expectations. Today, the memories from 1994 still play like a movie in my mind:

> My dad walking up the 18th fairway at the Old Course in the impossibly golden late afternoon sun, with both of us sure to break 80, smiling like he was in heaven.

> A tap-in eagle on the 14th at Carnoustie, receiving a quiet, "well-done" from my old Scottish caddy.

> Lunch in the Prestwick clubhouse, recounting each hole of that glorious and ancient links, shot by shot.

> The subtle, understated elegance of Panmure, designed by the great James Braid, where Ben Hogan practiced for the 1953 Open Championship.

These well-known links courses were brilliant, but it was the lesser-known spots that changed my entire outlook on the game of golf. The sincere welcome afforded to American visitors—and the genuine interest in golf, in clubhouse bars at Machrihanish, Cruden Bay, Machrie, and Brora—were a life-changing experience for me.

Our longest stay in any one place had been several nights at Ardell House, next to Machrihanish. Many nights at the Machrihanish bar, as I ordered a pint of Tennent's 70 Shilling, a complete stranger might ask, "How did you get on out there today?" A two-hour discussion on the merits of the links—and a friendly comparison to Dunaverty—was likely to ensue. There was a genuine interest in a visitor's thoughts and a pride of place that was remarkable. Those evenings—whether discussing the correct approach shot into "Bruach Mor," the 7th at Machrihanish, or the best line off the tee on "Whins," the 14th at Cruden Bay—were a joy.

Golf was and is a part of the fabric of life in Scotland. And the golf courses! This country, about the size of the American state of South Carolina, has 560 golf courses, one for every 9,500 people. There's no other place on earth that matches the quality of Scottish golf courses from top to bottom. The Kintyre Peninsula of Argyll and Bute, the Hebridean islands, and the Isle of Arran struck a chord in my heart that has never left me in almost 30 years. I have been fortunate to return many times.

The gravel car park at Dunaverty Golf Club was empty when we arrived. I walked over to the small, unassuming clubhouse to find that it was locked. There was a sign by the door:

GREEN FEES £5. PLACE IN HONESTY BOX.

This brought a smile to my face. My dad placed two £5 notes in the small box by the tee, and we looked around to find the fairway, but all we could see were grazing cattle and a few sheep. There were a few scorecards in the box, so we each studied one for clues. The course was a par 66 and a mere 4,799 yards. Starting to feel a bit skeptical of Mr. Baxter's recommendation, I saw a flag on the hill in the distance, with Dunaverty Rock and the Isle of Sanda stretching beyond. An entire herd of cows was grazing in the 1st and 18th fairways between us and the green.

"I think we are going to that flag up on the hill," I said. We then noticed another somewhat ominous sign to right of the 1st tee:

WARNING
ELECTRIFIED FENCES AT
1st, 2nd, 3rd, 4th, 17th & 18th GREENS
PLEASE TAKE CARE

Our opening drives somehow avoided the massive, black-and-white cattle that were completely oblivious to the small projectiles flying among them. Other than the herd of cows, which were kept off the small, square greens by the electric fences, the first two holes were straightforward. When we reached the 3rd tee, I started to understand why we had been sent here. From the 3rd to the 11th, we played the most fun and scenic stretch of golf holes that I had ever seen. The blind punchbowl, par three 4th hole was a particular highlight, with my dad nearly holing out from the tee. On the 5th tee, I said quietly, almost to myself, "I can't believe this place."

Hole after hole was like my perfect ideal dream of golf. Greens were located in dells and hollows, high above the golden beach, often hidden by massive dunes. The ball rolled and rolled along the ground, only stopping when it ran out of energy. My dad played inspired golf, adding a birdie on the par three 7th to go out in 32 strokes. After he made yet another birdie two on the 10th hole, called Mount Zion, we were both having the day of our lives. Reaching the oblivious cattle again on the 18th fairway, my lifelong playing partner only needed a par four for a career best round of 66. After his textbook par, we shook hands, and I looked at my watch. I realized it was only 3:30 pm. We had just played Dunaverty in less than three hours, yet it had never seemed like we were in a hurry. I wanted to go back around again. We did. The 1st tee was a mere few steps from the 18th green.

"Should we put 10 more pounds in the box?," my dad asked.

"Yes, we better," I said.

I saw David Baxter at breakfast the next morning. He came up and asked me, "How did you get along at Dunaverty?"

"We loved it. It was so much fun," I answered. "Just a beautiful place."

"Aye," was all he said, with a smile.

We played Machrihanish again that day, our last round of that seminal trip, before making our way back to the Glasgow airport. As we were leaving, I left my copy of *To the Linksland* in the main hall of Ardell House, along with a thank-you note to Mr. Baxter. In the clubhouse, I got an application to join Machrihanish from their club secretary, Anna Anderson. A few months later, Mr. Baxter signed it for me as a reference, and I became a member of Machrihanish Golf Club.

I returned many times in the ensuing years, playing in club competitions and meeting many great people. On each visit to the Kintyre Peninsula, my heart was taken more and more by the links at Dunaverty. It was the place that I thought about the most in those years when I could not visit Scotland. I dreamed of playing there one day with my own boys. At holiday gatherings, my father and I often talked about that perfect day in 1994.

In May 2019, I made it back to Dunaverty for the first time in several years, this time with my 25-year-old middle son, Jake. On that same simple, perfectly unchanged 1st tee, we met a friend from Twitter: Robbie Wilson of nearby Lochgilphead. We had a perfect afternoon of golf, much like that day almost exactly 25 years before. The cows welcomed our return as they dutifully guarded the first green. Jake laughed out loud when he saw the 4th green. On the 9th hole, he drove the blind green and made eagle, laughing once again as we came over the ridge and saw his ball not far from the flag. The gorse was an explosion of yellow all over the course. Robbie was the perfect host, giving us the lines on every shot and offering to take our photo together several times. He was like a walking history lesson, whether discussing the ancient standing stone on the 13th hole or the site of Dunaverty Castle in the distance. We immediately became friends. I was struck, perhaps even more so than on previous visits, at the stunning natural beauty of Dunaverty. I felt at home.

Standing in the car park after our round, on a sunny Scottish spring afternoon, we all promised to meet there again one day. I mentioned that maybe next time I could bring my youngest son Jordan along, a budding college golfer.

"Aye, that would be lovely, Jim. You'll be back, no doubt," Robbie said.

After I got home to Alabama a few weeks later, my new friend helped me join Dunaverty Golf Club, much like Mr. Baxter had done so many years before at Machrihanish. Jake and I immediately started talking about our next trip, and Jordan seemed interested in the possibility of joining us.

Robbie and I became increasingly close friends over the next several months, even more so as the onset of Covid in early 2020 seemed to make the world grow continually smaller. We often discussed places in Scotland that we'd like to play together. Around that time, my writing career finally started to see some success. I had a story published on Dunaverty in *The Links Diary*, a new Scottish golf journal. *The Golfer's Journal*—perhaps the world's best golf publication—had accepted one of my stories. I'd send Robbie potential itineraries for our next trip, with remote places like Askernish, Isle of Harris, and Iona always listed along with our must-visits, Dunaverty and Machrihanish.

A return trip was fully booked for May 2020 but was canceled due to the pandemic. Months prior, everyone had said, *surely it will all be over by May*. Like most people around the world, much of life was put on hold. Each time a return trip would get canceled, I'd start the planning process over again.

On the positive side, the pandemic gave me more time at home to finish my first book. Life was far from perfect, but it was good.

In early August 2021, I would finally meet my friend again in Lochgilphead, on the west coast of Scotland. The reason for the visit was too terrible to comprehend.

2 JORDAN

"My only prayer is, if I can't be there
Lord, protect my child"
—Bob Dylan, "Lord Protect My Child"

I'll never forget the moment when I decided to go all in on my son Jordan's golf career. It was in the final round of the 12- and 13-year-old division of the Alabama State Junior Championship at the classic Donald Ross-designed Mountain Brook Club, just outside of Birmingham. There had been a two-hour rain delay, with only a few holes left to play for the leaders. As we sat in the exceedingly formal MBC clubhouse waiting out the violent summer thunderstorms, Jordan and I discussed his chances. He was three strokes back. He was only 12—still at an age that sitting and talking with his father at a golf tournament with his friends around wasn't a complete embarrassment. Jordan had always been the most positive kid I knew, and he was no different this day. "If I birdie the last three holes," he smiled, "I still have a chance, Dad."

When play finally resumed, the boys went right back out to their positions with no warm-up. Jordan's first hole was a difficult 170-yard par three, all over water, to a tiny green with an impossible pin location. I was up ahead watching by the green, as I always did in those precious years. My son was up first. He took a couple practice swings and played quickly. I can still hear the sound of that strike. The ball flew dead straight, landed two feet short of the hole, hit the pin and stopped on the edge of the cup. Right there I knew that I would do whatever possible—financial and personal concerns be damned—to help my son play golf at the highest level. I spent the next seven years of my life focused on this promise.

It was August 2, 2012, and Jordan shot the low round of the tournament that day, but he finished tied for second. The top 10 finishers that year all went on to play Division 1 collegiate golf. Many of them are still playing at various schools around the country. My sweet, happy boy—whose golf instructor once told me had more raw talent than any player he had ever taught—died on May 17, 2021, of an accidental drug overdose. He was just 21.

The grief of losing a child is not imaginable, comprehensible, describable, or quantifiable. It comes in waves and never really leaves; it arrives in subtle and devious forms. Just seeing Jordan's blue KPMG golf hat—he was a huge Phil Mickelson fan—could make me cry uncontrollably for an hour. A few days after his death, we opened a safe in his room. It contained two letters from his former high school golf teammates, a Jalen Hurts football card, and various photos of our family together over the years, including one of me holding him at the hospital the day he was born. It was heartbreaking beyond comprehension. I was barely able to get out of bed most days and found it almost impossible to focus on my work as an architect. The sense of guilt I felt over Jordan's death—and would probably always feel—was often overwhelming.

Not long after his run at the State Junior Championship, Jordan began to take lessons from the well-known teacher Hank Johnson at Greystone Golf Club in Birmingham. The lessons were wildly expensive, but I didn't care. Jordan loved Hank and his game was improving all the time. He was named Player of the Year by the Alabama Junior Golf Association and started playing on the varsity team at Hartselle High School in 7th grade. In the summer, our family vacations were spent traveling to tournaments all over the southeast. By 2013, still in 8th grade, he was one of the top players on a talented high school golf team. He won two events that year and three more the following year. The team qualified for the state high school championship in 2013 and finished third in 2014.

In 2015, Jordan was a sophomore, and the best player on a stacked team. There was a special chemistry and determination with that group and rural, small town Hartselle High School won the Alabama state championship over two teams from the Birmingham area that were loaded with Shoal Creek and Country Club of Birmingham members. After the final hole, he was ecstatic and hugged me harder and longer than any other time in his life. It remains the single happiest moment of my time on earth.

But time does not stop. Although three of that core group of golfers were back in 2016, the team chemistry had changed. Jordan still had a great individual season. He was happy, made good grades and won two more times that spring. I bought him his first car. College coaches began to contact him, including two Division I programs in Alabama. We took a visit to one of the schools the summer following his junior year. After talking to Jordan for 10 minutes, the coach offered him a scholarship. He was so proud and happy. I was too. What father would not be overjoyed? Jordan had already been offered a full golf scholarship to a local two-year college, so we told the coach we were going to think about it. Division I golf and academics are tough, so I wanted us to consider all the choices—maybe starting out at a smaller school would be better for him.

Jordan and I had high hopes for his senior golf season in 2017. He'd had a good summer, making the cut in the Future Masters and playing well in several other events. He practiced every day until dark, and it showed. I'd sit on our front porch in the evenings and wait for him to get home from the course so he could tell me about his day. I can remember listening for the sound of his car coming up the street. He was the team leader now. All the guys that he had played with for so many years were gone.

In hindsight, I think this started to affect him. Those friends had always been a positive influence on him, but his new group didn't have the same vibe. His grades slipped badly. He said he was having a hard time concentrating on his schoolwork. He was really worried about it, and we found him a respected psychiatrist. He was prescribed Adderall. I believe this is the first, but maybe most critical factor, that ultimately led to his death.

In my opinion, Adderall is a dangerous drug. While I'm sure it has helped a lot of people, it's also widely abused on high school and college campuses. I still wonder if he was encouraged by friends at school to try to get a prescription for it. But at the time, we didn't think much of it, because Jordan's grades improved almost immediately. He appeared happy and said he could focus so much better at school. His wonderful high school golf coach praised him for the academic improvement. Everything seemed to be back on track. That proved to be a high watermark; his happy, outgoing personality began to change over the next few months.

Jordan still had a good senior season. He mentored the younger players and the team played well, although not at the heights of the previous years. Jordan was just not quite himself. He started to become more withdrawn at home. Gone were the conversations of the summer—he would go in his room and shut the door when he got home from golf practice. Although he won once and made several all-tournament teams that season, as I look back at all the photos from that season now, some of the sparkle had left his eyes.

But there were still some wonderful moments. The team made it through sectionals and was on to sub-state, where only the top two teams advanced to the state championship. Jordan wasn't striking it well that day but battled the entire round and managed a 74. After finishing third as a team, his high school career was over.

Life has so many abrupt endings. We think things will go on forever, but they do not. The winning team was full of guys that had been Jordan's rivals for almost six years. As they were celebrating by the 18th green, my son walked over into the middle of them and shook every single one of their hands. I still cry when thinking about it. I think I always will.

Jordan graduated from high school in May 2017. I look at his senior photographs now and don't know why I didn't do more to help him. He played his last Future Masters and Alabama State Junior that summer before college. Even though he played decently, I knew something was wrong. He didn't prepare the way he had always done. We decided that it would be best to accept the community college scholarship. The Division I coach understood and made it clear Jordan could still come play for him after his first year. It seemed like a good plan. But the community college coach who had signed him, who knew Jordan well and loved him, quit before the season started. A totally different coach, with a style of negative reinforcement, took over. That was the absolute worst thing that could've happened, given Jordan's fragile mental state. He quit school and college golf after the second golf tournament.

We didn't talk much for several months afterward. It was frightening, but he was still seeing the same psychiatrist, so I thought he would eventually be okay. Sure enough, after those tough months, he surprised me by proclaiming he wanted to play golf again. He was so talented, another community college in the area immediately offered him a full scholarship. It seemed like he was returning to his old self. He started practicing and going to see his instructor again. I took him to the school and got him signed up for all his classes.

I know he was trying really hard to make it. We began talking more. When his new team started the fall season in 2019, Jordan was so excited. I played a few rounds with him at Sweetens Cove in those weeks leading up to September, and he played brilliant golf. He had a 30 on one nine-hole loop. I was letting myself believe that my son had come back to the world. I did not see any major issues, but in the back of my mind I knew he still acted somewhat off at times—"Adderall strange" is the only way I know to phrase it. He had to pass random drug testing to play, so he wasn't taking anything illegal at the time. That made me feel better.

The team qualified each week for upcoming tournaments, like most schools do. After playing decent golf with a few stretches of brilliance in the first event, he missed qualifying for the second one. I have since learned that the coach chewed him out in front of the entire team after that first tournament—yelling that he had "wasted a scholarship" on him. But he got back after it and led the first round of qualifying the following week with a 69. After the round, instead of being praised for having a great day, his coach asked why he didn't play that way all the time. Jordan told his mother all of this; I never knew any of it until after his death. I am now sure he suffered from severe anxiety, low self-esteem, and at least moderate depression. Considering that, the negativity of his new coach was dangerously unhealthy for Jordan. I am not placing blame on the man, but it was the exact opposite approach Jordan needed. Two days after that 69, Jordan quit school and college golf again.

After leaving college golf for the second time, Jordan began to slip further away from us. He quit playing altogether and rarely spoke to me. He had a girlfriend at the time and when she broke up with him unexpectedly, he withdrew even further. He rarely left his room, staying up all night playing video games and sleeping all day. I suspected that he might have started experimenting with other drugs besides Adderall, but I didn't know what to do. I'd occasionally text him that I loved him and would do anything to help him. He would sometimes respond with "I love you, too, Dad," but that was about the extent of our interaction during that time.

A ray of hope broke through when he decided to work on the grounds crew at the local golf club where he learned to play the game with my father. His first ever tournament win was the junior club championship there when he was just 12 years old, beating players that were several years older than him. I wondered about him going to work there after having been a member for so long, but he seemed to love it. He was far from himself, but he got up every morning, went to work, and worked hard. Many mornings he would send pictures of a fairway or green he had just finished mowing to his mother, brothers, and me on our group text. I started to talk to him about pursuing a career in golf course maintenance.

In late fall 2020, he lost his job unexpectedly at the golf course. The reasons why are not important. He loved being on the greens crew and was proud of his work. This job loss was catastrophic for his mental state and sense of self-worth. I believe it was the final blow that he could not fully recover from. He retreated to his room and back to playing Playstation all night and sleeping all day. We rarely spoke. I knew he was either drinking heavily and/or taking drugs of some kind. I did not know what to do. He was 21 years old. I could not make him do anything that he did not want to do.

Early in 2021, he made some small attempts to engage with the family. He went to play nine holes with his two older brothers. One Sunday in February, he sat down and watched golf with me for two hours. His eyes were clear, and he was smiling. He continued working on a one-hole golf course he had started building in our backyard when he had been on the greens crew. Despite these flashes, there were still so many times when I could tell something was off. Nevertheless, I remained hopeful. We watched the Masters together that spring for the first time in years. In late April, he played in a big golf tournament with me at the University of Alabama. We talked the entire drive there. Our group included one of his heroes, former Alabama quarterback A.J. McCarron. Jordan's swing still looked perfect, and he played well that day. McCarron asked him for swing advice. We had a great time, but when I looked at his eyes, I could see he was still struggling.

I was working in my office in early May when Jordan knocked on the door and came in. He never did that. He said excitedly, "Dad, I know I have wasted my talent these last few years. I want to play golf again. I want to play in tournaments again. I can try the mini tours." I was shocked. I told him I didn't care if he ever played golf again, but if that's what he wanted, I'd help. He would not stop: "I know I can do it, Dad. I'm ready to work at it again." Thrilled that he was talking to me again, I went along with it. For the last 10 days of his life, we spoke every day. We talked seriously about him joining me and Jake for our next trip to Scotland. We watched golf videos at night and talked about Mickelson's chances at the PGA. I laughed and said Phil had no chance, but Jordan thought he might play well. He went to play golf with his grandfather, my dad, on May 12. He texted me shot by shot, something he had not done since his junior year of high school: "Just had four feet for birdie." "Eagle putt on 5 lipped out." "This is the best I've hit the ball in four years." "I just shot 70 and it should have been a 63." "I know I can come back." I let myself think that maybe he was getting better.

In the aftermath, you analyze every moment you can remember of the final days. On May 14, the Friday before Jordan died, I had driven to Jacksonville State University in northeast Alabama for a work project. On my way back home, he texted me: "Can you give me some money to buy a practice net to put in the backyard? I've been chipping all day, but I want to work on my swing." Of course I would. When I got home, he was in the front yard waiting for me. I gave him $40, and he thanked me. He returned a few minutes later with a net that he immediately erected in the backyard. That afternoon, I was in my home office when I got another text from him: "Can you come out here and take some videos of my swing?" He had not asked me to do this since his senior year in high school. It was a late Spring evening in Alabama and his swing looked perfect.

The next day, Saturday, I bought him lunch at Zaxby's. He left at some point in the afternoon with a friend who had asked him to help on a potential landscaping project. I went to bed early to read a book. While I was lying in bed, I had the idea to take Jordan up to Sweetens Cove to play the next day. We had not been there together in a long time. Out the window, in the twilight, I saw him cutting the small green in our backyard with a manual reel mower. He had his headphones on, so I went back to bed and fell asleep before texting him about playing. It was the last time I saw my son alive.

On Sunday around 9 am, I texted him about playing. He responded immediately: "I would love to, Dad, but we are going to work on this landscaping project today. I am going to get paid $100." He seemed proud to be doing some work and making a little money on his own, so I did not push it: "Okay, be careful. I will see you when I get home tonight. I love you."

"Love you too," he responded. It was our last communication.

I made the drive up to my favorite American golf course and walked 18 holes. When I got home that night, Jordan wasn't there. My wife said he was still working. Exhausted from the day, I went to sleep, thinking that it was good that he was doing something he enjoyed. The next morning, Monday, May 17, I took a shower to get ready for a 9 am Zoom meeting. Afterward, I saw a notice on my phone that a 9-1-1 call had been made from Jordan's number at 8:16. It was approximately 8:20 when I saw it. I went straight to his room, which was out in our old garage and a little separate from the rest of the house. He wasn't there. I immediately called my wife, who was at our oldest son's house babysitting our new grandson. She told me Jordan had come in late to get his Playstation. He had taken it over to his grandfather's house, who was out of town, to play with his friend. They had just decided to stay there together and play video games all night.

I called Jordan's phone. No answer. I rushed to my dad's house, which is less than a five-minute drive away. There's no point in describing what I saw and what happened over the next several frantic minutes. It is something that no parent should ever see. It is my sincere prayer that any parent reading this never has to experience it. At the hospital they told us that Jordan had likely died from an interaction between Adderall and an opioid pill or Xanax, possibly laced with fentanyl. There was no alcohol in his system.

The days following my son's death were a blur. Thankfully there were some kind family members who handled most of the arrangements. I asked two of Jordan's state championship teammates and his high school golf coach to be pallbearers. I wrote Jordan's obituary:

> *Jordan Hartsell, age 21, died suddenly and unexpectedly on May 17, 2021. He was a sweet boy with a good heart. He loved his family, especially his grandfather Lee, and his dog Champ. He was one of the best junior golfers in the state of Alabama and was*

a member of the 2015 6A State Championship team for Hartselle High School, which he graduated from in 2017. Jordan played on the varsity team at HHS for 6 years and won several individual tournaments during that time. He signed a golf scholarship with Calhoun and had offers from several Division 1 schools. He loved golf from the time he was a small boy and he loved playing with his dad, who taught him the game. He loved the beach and family trips to Gulf Shores every summer. He also loved Alabama Crimson Tide football and basketball.

He is survived by his mother Jaymaine, who he was very close to, and his father Jim. He is also survived by his two older brothers, Jonathan Hartsell and Jake Hartsell, who loved him and watched over him fiercely when he was little. He is survived by his grandparents Lee (who he loved unconditionally) and June Hartsell and Joel Ward and Danny Wiley. He loved his new nephew Otis Hartsell and was so proud of him.

There will be a graveside service at 11 AM on Thursday, May 20 at Hartselle City Cemetery. Pallbearers will be Zac Ward, Jeremiah Rhodes, Joshua Rhodes, Garrett Reist, Jake Tiffin, and Coach Chad Gladden. In lieu of flowers, we ask that you consider donating to youthoncourse.org in Jordan's memory.

For several weeks after that horrific day, the final editing and completion of my book *The Secret Home of Golf* occupied much of my time and, more importantly, my mind. I tried to find out and understand what had happened to my son, but soon realized that we would never actually know for sure. The first time the supposed friend who was with Jordan that last night doesn't tell a lie will be the first time that he has ever told the truth about anything. The 9-1-1 call from Jordan's phone haunted me. Had he made the call? His phone was found in his pocket, switched off. I had recurring nightmares about it. A discussion with the E911 director revealed that the call lasted two seconds and then was ended, with no words spoken. The emergency operator attempted to call his number several times, but it went straight to voicemail. I called the county coroner, then went to the police department to see if anything could be done to investigate further. There were no answers, only more questions. You would think it might help to know exactly what happened, but I wasn't sure it would. With the final edits of the book completed in June, I was just trying to make it day to day. It was rare for me to sleep for more than an hour at a time.

The death of a child hijacks your memories. Death holds them hostage. Those precious moments I had spent the last 20 years collecting with Jordan were suddenly a bad thing. They caused severe pain. I had thousands of photographs and videos of my son's years of playing golf: smiling with his friends, holding trophies, with his grandfather or me. Every time I saw one, or some well-meaning person sent me something, it was a terrible reminder of what I had lost—what we all had lost. I did not know what to say when a stranger asked me if I had any children. In the entire time since his passing, I had gone into his bedroom twice. It was so overwhelming; I couldn't do it anymore. Every part of my being and life was affected. All the memories that had been my greatest source of pride and joy now caused distress.

My family was struggling as much as I was. Our new grandson, Otis, offered some level of comfort to Jaymaine, my wife. I was glad that she had him to spend time with, and I know it helped some, but with his curly blond hair he looked a lot like Jordan had at that age. Seeing Otis was also a constant reminder of what she had just lost. Her darkest moments were probably worse than mine, if that's possible. I spent a lot of time talking to my oldest son, Jonathan. We would drive around the back roads of Morgan County, Alabama, talking about Jordan. They had experienced a slight falling out a few months earlier, and I could tell that it haunted him. We each constantly questioned what we could have done differently—and the insane tragic string of occurrences that had to fall in line for this to happen.

My middle son, Jake, had been one of the main reasons I survived the horrific days just after Jordan's death. He did everything for us and physically kept me from falling on the ground at the funeral. When they were both little, Jake had been fiercely protective of his little curly-headed brother. In almost every photo we have, Jake has his arm around Jordan like he never wanted to let him go. I was very concerned about him. He lived by himself about an hour away from us. I worried that he had been in complete shock that first week and was just now feeling the impact of the crushing grief.

We all grieve differently. I had to do something drastic. I was fortunate that they all supported me on what I felt I needed to do to survive. It would be a sacrifice for them.

On August 2, 2021—exactly nine years to the day of that long ago junior golf tournament—I boarded a plane by myself in Huntsville, Alabama, to fly to Glasgow, Scotland, to spend a month in my favorite country. This time in Scotland would be my seventh visit to the kingdom. I had to find out if there was a way to continue with a life that felt destroyed. It seemed like the only way to begin to heal from the unhealable. I wanted to attempt to reclaim the memories of my precious son. Golf had been the framework of our life—a source of so much joy—maybe it could reveal something that I could not see through the crushing grief.

3 ROBBIE

Smiles in the sunshine and tears in the rain
Still take me back where my memories remain
Flickering embers grow higher and higher
As they carry me back to the Mull of Kintyre

—Paul McCartney & Wings, "Mull of Kintyre"

On my previous visit in 2019 to the Mull of Kintyre—a now generally accepted name for the southern tip of the peninsula that makes up a large part of Argyll & Bute on the west coast of Scotland—my son Jake and I had played that memorable round of golf at Dunaverty with Robbie Wilson. He lived just up the A83 from Campbeltown in the lochside town of Lochgilphead. I had met Robbie through Twitter, initially following him because of his wonderful photos of ancient historic sites in western Scotland. His posts were fascinating, showing a herd of red deer at Lochranza Castle or an ancient stone circle on a windswept moor in Kilmartin Glen. Before too long, it became obvious that he was also an avid golfer and a member of Machrihanish Golf Club: one of my favorite places. I was a member there from 1994 to 2010.

In all my trips over the years, I always returned to the Kintyre peninsula. No matter if I went as far north to Cruden Bay, Brora, or even Reay, I would inevitably plan to spend several days in the Machrihanish area. In my mind, Machrihanish is the original "Secret Home of Golf." I often referred to it that way after my first visit in 1994, and that is where the idea for the title of my first book originated. Robbie and I corresponded on Twitter for several weeks prior to our visit. The plan was for the three of us to play Machrihanish and Dunaverty together while we were staying in Campbeltown at the Ardshiel Hotel.

I had fallen in love with Argyll on that first visit with my dad almost 30 years ago. It always felt a little like coming home. The golf, the history, the wonderful people, and the hauntingly beautiful landscape had much to do with those feelings, but somehow the connection seemed deeper than that. I've never been that interested in ancient family history, but a search on a genealogy website a few years ago indicated I had a direct ancestor from Castleton—only three miles from Lochgilphead—who immigrated to America in the late 1700s. Maybe there's something in my DNA that has drawn me back to Argyll and Kintyre so many times. I have always felt that something about being in Scotland opens your mind to the more mystical and spiritual side of life.

It can be argued that Argyll is the cradle of history in Scotland. The coast is separated from Ireland by only 12 miles of the Irish Sea. In around 500 AD, a group of people who came over the Irish Sea to Scotland built a vast network of hill forts at Dunadd, near Kilmartin. At that time, Argyll was much more accessible from the northern coast of Ireland than from the rest of the Scottish countryside. These fortifications in Kilmartin Glen are the earliest embryos of Scotland coming together as an organized state. Around the same time, Christianity was first brought over the sea to Scotland by Saint Columba, who is said to have landed in Southend, near where Dunaverty Golf Club is located today.

As Jake and I made our way around the east coast in May 2019—visiting Elie, Anstruther, St. Andrews, Cruden Bay, Fraserburgh, Cullen, and Covesea—Robbie and I talked frequently. He wanted to know details of the various courses we were playing. He was always keenly interested in how we got on with our dining and hotel choices at night. As we edged closer to the Kintyre portion of the itinerary, he asked me—I'm not sure why—if we could play Dunaverty together instead of Machrihanish.

It was a day I will never forget. Robbie was a perfect host, pointing out the correct lines and giving us an ongoing history lesson about Dunaverty Castle, Robert the Bruce, and the ancient Brunerican standing stone just off the 13th fairway at Dunaverty. I was fascinated by his job, which involved looking after several ancient and prehistoric sites on the west coast and islands for Historic Environment Scotland. He graciously—and without us asking—took several photos of Jake, myself, and Kaylin, Jake's long-time girlfriend who had made the trip with us. These are photos I treasure now.

As sometimes happens in life, especially through the game of golf, Robbie and I hit it off immediately that day and had since become close friends. I became a member of Dunaverty, my favorite course in the world, with his help. He was one of the first people I contacted about Jordan's death. I didn't want him to see something about it first on social media. We spoke, with me not able to get out many coherent words, and Robbie offered to do anything he could to help. We didn't talk very long, but the tone of his voice conveyed a deep and real sense of pain that I will never forget.

A few weeks after that terrible call, I started thinking seriously about trying to get away to Scotland for a month. A previously planned trip—which was to include Jake, and possibly Jordan—had been canceled because of the pandemic. I didn't know if there's a way to break the pattern of day-to-day crippling grief, but I had to try something. My office had graciously told me to take as much time off as I needed. Even so, there's no way I could afford a trip of that magnitude without some serious help. I sent Robbie a message and asked him if I could talk to him about something. We agreed to talk the next night after he got home from work.

"How ya' doing, Jim?"

"I need to ask you something, Robbie. Can I come stay at your house in August for—", and he cut me off before I could go any further.

"Stop right there. You'll stay at mine as long as you need to. It's no bother. I'll take off work when I can, and we'll play golf."

We talked a bit more about the dates and the potential problems with Covid travel requirements. He wanted to know how my family was coping, especially Jake. Robbie was hopeful that the restrictions might be reduced soon. If not, I'd likely spend the first eight days of my trip quarantining in his back garden in Lochgilphead. The following night, I sent him my proposed itinerary for the month. Due to the uncertainty, much of the first two weeks was loosely organized and open-ended, with his home as a base. "Brilliant, Jim. You'll have plenty of places to go," he responded.

My oldest son Jonathan dropped me off at the small but highly efficient Huntsville, Alabama airport early on the morning of August 1. I started to cry as he hugged me and said, "Be careful, Dad. I love you." He had been my rock since Jordan's death.

The flights, with stops in Chicago and Amsterdam, were uneventful. People seemed genuinely happy to be traveling again. It was a trip I had made many times over the years, but this was the first time I'd be traveling alone. I missed Jake's excitement and anticipation from the previous flight to Scotland. Less than two days before I was to leave, the Scottish government lifted the quarantine requirement for American travelers. Suddenly, if I could just test negative for Covid after arrival, I'd have nine days of free travel on the west coast of Scotland.

My mind had been racing about places I had never been able to visit. The anticipation of something is half the fun of doing it.

The nice young woman at the Hertz rental counter at Glasgow airport was ecstatic to hear my Alabama accent. "You are the first American I've seen in almost two years," she said with a huge smile.

"You're here for a month? On holiday or for work?"

"A bit of both, I think. Scotland is my favorite country," I replied.

"Aye, it's lovely, isn't it?," she said, as she handed me the keys to a hybrid Toyota. Her voice was like hearing an old friend. I felt strangely at peace for the first time since May 17th. I was on my way home.

The drive over the Erskine Bridge and around Loch Lomond on the A82 to Lochgilphead is one I've made many times—it's a beautiful stretch along the loch, past the historic village of Luss, with its ancient granite and slate architecture. I could see Loch Lomond Golf Club through the tall Scots pines. Past Luss came the village of Tarbet and mighty Ben Lomond: the Hill of the Beacon. The striking stone facade of the Tarbet Hotel faces the intersection of the A82 and A85, where you must decide to head north to Crianlarich or west to Inverary. The road was surprisingly busy, with camper vans and cars jamming the car park across from the hotel. I stopped and found a bench in a smooth green field by the famous lake, celebrated throughout history in poetry and song. I looked over the water and mountains and thought about my son. I replayed the last week of his life, as I did in almost every free minute. It had become almost like a sad ritual—one in which I hoped some answer would finally reveal itself. There were families with small children having picnics on the shore.

I felt a sharp pang of grief as I watched a young father kick a soccer ball back and forth with his small son. An old grainy video from Gulf Links—a homemade public course on the Alabama coast that Jordan loved to play when he was young—suddenly played in my head. It was just the two of us, and he was only six years old. We had gone out early to avoid the oppressive gulf-coast humidity. Jordan had made his first-ever par, and I recorded his reaction in the golf cart. The short clip, which I had managed to keep for almost 15 years, ended with him saying, "I love you, Dad." As I got up from the bench, my legs nearly buckled. The sky was crystal-clear blue, with the sun illuminating everything in a surreal yellow light. I walked to the car and drove on to Lochgilphead.

Robbie greeted me in his tidy shop with a hug. "You'll be needing some tea," he said. He returned with some cakes and two cups. It was such a relief to simply talk about golf with him. We discussed where I should go for the first part of the trip. He planned to join me for as much as he was able. We would, of course, play Dunaverty and Machrihanish together, but I convinced him to come with me out to the remote Isle of Colonsay to play the ancient course there. It's a two-and-a-half-hour ferry ride from Oban. There's one hotel with eight rooms. We booked one before the tea cooled.

Robbie seemed excited about the possibilities: "There is a wee plane that flies from Oban to Colonsay, if you can't book the ferry. I think it might actually land on the golf course," he said with a laugh. My friend had a few more hours to work, so he told me to go on to his house and get settled in. "Do I need a key to get in?," I asked.

"No, no need to lock my door in Lochgilphead," he answered. My pre-ordered Covid test was waiting for me at his house, along with an already addressed and posted return package. I administered the test, and then I called Robbie to ask where the nearest red Royal Mail post box was. "There is one on the path into town. I'll take it for you when I get home, no bother. I can get us some fish and chips for dinner." By 10 am the next morning, I received the test result via email: negative.

We ate takeaway fish and chips from the Argyll Café that night and watched golf on Sky Sports. (A good meal of fish and chips in Scotland is one of the top 10 pleasures in life. Like a pint of Tennent's, it's just not something that will ever taste the same in the USA, despite the best efforts of chefs and bartenders.) Robbie never once mentioned the tragedy that had brought on my visit. I think he wanted me to have some sense of normalcy, and he was right. He had to work the next day, so I'd be on my own. Before heading upstairs to bed, I mentioned that I might go play at Tarbert Golf Club, a nine-holer about 20 minutes away, if I passed my Covid test. "Aye, that will test your legs. You can have breakfast at Café Ca'Dora in Tarbert."

As I would find throughout those first 10 days I stayed at my friend's house, his recommendations—and editorial comments—

were always spot-on. The sausage and egg roll at Café Ca'Dora was excellent. Fresh bread is an art form in Scotland. After I finished my tea, I walked across the street and spent a few minutes sitting on my favorite bench at Tarbert Harbour. I had sat in this same spot with my dad, and once with Jake, when the world wasn't quite as sad and broken. In 1994, we bought fresh rolls and Mull of Kintyre cheddar and had a busman's lunch, looking at the boats sailing into Tarbert Harbour. In a world without Jordan, it now almost seemed unfair to recall these treasured memories. It had been less than three months since the funeral. My mind still could not fully grasp the magnitude of the destruction to our entire family.

Tarbert is a lovely town. The old stone buildings face the water, cascading down the hillside. The ruins of Tarbert Castle keep silent watch over it all, haunted by the ghosts of the Lords of the Isles. On the bench, the years came flooding back to me. This was the seventh time I had visited this beautiful peninsula. There was always such a sense of excitement and anticipation when I stopped in this spot, on my way to Dunaverty or Machrihanish. I sat here once again because it was what I had always done, maybe because I remembered how excited my dad had been so many years before. Did this ritual even mean the same thing now? Are you allowed to ever enjoy anything again after your child dies? Before I knew it, 30 minutes had passed.

It was a sunny day. I was in Kintyre. I suddenly felt the need to play golf. Jordan would want me to do that, I told myself.

In many ways, Tarbert Golf Club—located just outside of town on and above West Loch Tarbert—was the perfect place for me to ease myself back into the Scottish game. It has many of the elements— fun, quirkiness, natural beauty, and economy—that epitomize what I love about golf in this country. There's a small golf shed by the first tee where you drop your greens fee in an honesty box. As a member of Dunaverty, this was a nominal sum of £10 for me. There was no one around, and I parked my rented Toyota by the 1st tee, just a few feet from the shed, as Robbie had advised me to do.

After depositing the payment, I stood on the 1st tee and surveyed the scene. To the left of the tee, the dark blue loch stretched into the distance. There appeared to be a burn crossing the fairway about 180 yards from the tee. The 260-yard par four was flattish, but I was staring straight at the heights of Meall Mhòr as a backdrop. The summer had been dry throughout Scotland, so the course was a perfect shade of light-greenish brown. My semi-topped drive ran like a dog chasing a squirrel before it jumped the burn, leaving me a short pitch to the green. I couldn't help but smile at seeing a ball roll so far on the ground. This was the true game.

The 2nd hole, another fun, short par four, turns 90 degrees left of the 1st and runs along the base of the mountain. When I got to the 3rd tee, I finally understood Robbie's cryptic warning from the night before about Tarbert being a "test" for my legs. The 145-yard par three goes straight up the mountain. It's one of the most sheer, vertical climbs I have ever experienced on a golf course. Once this cliff is scaled, the 4th hole is another par three straight uphill, maybe only slightly less steep than its predecessor. When I reached the 5th tee, I was happy to see a bench. I sat down for several minutes and stared at the loch below.

Fortunately for my legs, the next three holes ran across the side slope of the Meall. The 5th hole, a 332-yard par four, would not be out of place at Gleneagles or Boat of Garten. A blind drive—over a burn flowing down quickly off the mountain—to a fairway that seems nonexistent. Golfers can see a lone tree in the distance that should be their aiming point. The green is tucked into a corner, perfectly situated at the base of another wooded incline. The 6th is a par four that returns parallel to the 5th and has a wonderful green site above the rushing burn.

At the par three 8th hole, golfers can finally wreak their revenge on the mountain. Called West Loch, it plays 128 yards with a sheer drop from the tee to the green of at least 130 feet. There was no wind to speak of, so a half-chipped wedge from the heights of the tee was sufficient to reach the semi-blind green below. There's a bell on the way to the 9th tee to signal that you've finished the hole. I rang it loudly as I walked by, although I appeared to be the only player on the course. Sometimes you just need to hear the bell pass through you and over the countryside.

The 9th hole plays along the B8024 back toward the small clubhouse and the 1st tee shed beyond. As I prepared to hit the short approach into the green, I first heard the laughter of—and then noticed—three young girls hitting balls into a large net between the clubhouse and the 9th green. The green site was lovely against a backdrop of wind-stunted trees. After holing out for a rare par, I walked back along the road to where my car was parked by the 1st tee. A large lorry full of baying sheep blocked my exit from the area.

Putting my clubs away, I looked over to the unconcerned lorry driver.

"Are ye' needing to get out? I won't be moving for quite a while. Drive around the wee shed. Nobody will mind."

My only exit path was to drive my car across the corner of the first tee, around the shed, through a small gap between the truck and the gorse. It looked questionable at best.

When I turned around, the three girls had made their way to the 1st tee, giggling loudly about something as they prepared to tee off. The smallest of them reached down to put her tee in the ground and declared, "I'm going to win today." She then hit a low line drive that stopped about 10 feet from the burn. I had no reason to doubt her prediction. The trio walked off quickly, almost running to their balls. That round at Gulf Links with Jordan quickly came back to me again. We had a cart that day, but he would sprint from one shot to the next until he reached the green. The memory was jarring, but I couldn't help but smile as the girls hit their second shots without a moment's hesitation.

When I got back to Robbie's place, he had just come in from work. "I thought I'd take you to see some of my sites around here. We can eat at the Kilmartin Hotel," said my friend. That evening I was treated to an incredible tour of ancient Kilmartin Glen. Robbie seemed rightfully proud of these remarkable historic sites that he's responsible for maintaining. The area was first settled in 5,000 BC. I'm sure my enthusiasm was obvious, as I said "wow" many times that night. My friend showed me around the entire Glen— ancient cairns, stone circles, and Carnasserie Castle. "You can't keep the

Outlander loons away from these standing stones now. They are mental," he said with a laugh. When we arrived at the hotel, next to Kilmartin Church and cemetery, it was getting dark, and a misting rain was falling over the glen. The temperature had dropped precipitously in just a few minutes.

The Kilmartin Hotel is one of those small country inns that you only seem to find in Scotland. A stark white exterior facade faces the somber burial ground, with granite grave slabs dating back centuries, across the road. The interior is all dark, polished wood with low ceilings. The bartender greeted Robbie warmly, by name, as we entered. We ordered our drinks at the bar—a pint of Tennent's for me and a Coke for the driver—and found a table. There was a peat fire burning. Several people had their dogs with them. The waitress told us about the evening specials. "Everything is good here, Jim," said my friend, "you can't really go wrong." The haggis nachos looked appealing, but so did the curry. I ordered another pint. We discussed ancient Scottish history late into the evening. Robbie never brought up the tragic reason why I was in Kilmartin Glen, over 3,200 miles from home. The gift of a moment of normalcy was priceless.

4

THE BRIDGE OVER THE ATLANTIC

Oh, golf is for smellin' heather and cut grass and walkin' fast across the countryside and feelin' the wind and watchin' the sun go down and seein' yer friends hit good shots and hittin' some yerself.

—Agatha McNaughton in Michael Murphy's *Golf in the Kingdom*

The Clachan Bridge, also grandly named "Bridge Over the Atlantic," takes you over to the Isle of Seil, and it's barely wide enough for one car. The camber is such that on this beautiful, 19th-century structure, you are driving completely blind as you proceed almost vertically up the steep, arched roadway. After I survived crossing the ancient bridge on a cold, cloudy morning, on the way out to play Isle of Seil Golf Club, I realized that you must have faith to drive over the bridge, trusting that the way is clear. There's no traffic signal. You can see nothing coming toward you as you start up the incline. It felt fitting for this trip, which required a similar leap of faith and hope.

During dinner at the Kilmartin the night before, Robbie and I had discussed my plans. He was scheduled to head off to work on some remote, uninhabited island at a prehistoric site, and he would be gone most of the day. "You should go to Isle of Seil. That place is right up your alley. You will love it. After you're done, go eat lunch at the café in Ellenabeich and take the wee ferry out to Easdale. That's you set for tomorrow," he had said confidently. Who was I to question such a directive?

One of the benefits of playing the lesser-known courses in Scotland is that your itinerary can be flexible. You don't need any tee times at most places—not likely that anyone would be around to arrange them for you anyway. Most golf clubs out this far on the west coast simply allow golfers to put their greens fee in the honesty box and go play. In this case of Isle of Seil, Robbie had also advised me that the store just down the street would also accept greens fees. I was in no hurry to get to the course, so I pulled over at the small car park just over the Clachan Bridge. I walked over to the edge of the slope and smiled quietly at the "Atlantic" below. It was a river that looked to be about 25 yards wide. A quick look at Google Maps showed that it's the (very narrow) Sound of Seil, which does indeed connect to larger bodies of water in the Atlantic. Seil is an island, if only by the smallest of geographical margins.

There were a few picnic tables with a nice view of the bridge, so I sat down. I was curious to watch and see if there were any issues with opposing cars meeting at the apex of the span. After about 10 minutes, I had not seen another single car pass by. Maybe the odds of two opposing drivers reaching the bridge simultaneously are so small that it's not a concern. Grief can take over the mind at any moment. It seemed to help at times to concentrate on even the most mundane things. Google Maps was still open on my phone.

There had been so many changes in the world since I first started visiting the west coast of Scotland 27 years ago. There were no cell phones—not to even mention satellite navigation—in 1994. I can still see my dad with a huge, unwieldy Ordnance Survey map of western Scotland—trying to give me directions to Machrihanish from the Glasgow airport— while I was trying to learn to drive a car with a steering wheel on the right. It's a fun memory now, but there were several near misses and many wrong turns. We stopped more than once to ask bemused locals for directions. Trying to navigate around Scotland, by yourself, in the days before smart phones was quite a challenge for visitors. It's much simpler to travel now—especially through the larger cities like Glasgow and Edinburgh—but I miss the wonderful Ordnance Survey maps of Scotland with their contours and elevations. Technology has made the world easier, but much less magical in some ways.

Isle of Seil Golf Club is located about three miles from the Clachan Bridge along the single-track B844 road. At the turn-off to the course, I stopped at the Balvicar store on the corner. It reminded me of a small convenience store in the US, but this one here had a post office. Orange Lucozade has long been my beverage of choice while walking the links of Scotland. I grabbed a Mars bar and two bottles of the neon sports drink and put them on the counter.

"Hiya! Will this be all for you?," asked the friendly cashier.

"Well, can I pay for the golf here?"

"Aye. Aye, you can. Let me get the book. Let's see, it's £10 for nine holes or £15 for a day ticket."

"Just the 9, I think. I'm going out to Easdale this afternoon."

"Aye. Brilliant spot. You'll enjoy that," she said, handing me a scorecard and a bag tag showing that my greens fee was paid in full.

The small gravel car park, next to the golf shed, was empty when I arrived. Painted a bright teal green—and boldly emblazoned with "ISLE OF SEIL GOLF CLUB"—the golf hut is a work of art. I looked inside and read several of the club notices tacked to the walls, which included a simple diagram of the course layout. There was an old church pew on one side of the room, acting as a bench. A solitary pushcart was parked in the middle of the room. Smiling, I signed the guest book ceremoniously, thinking a little proudly to myself, "I wonder how many people from Alabama have ever been here?"

Today would be the second of many solo rounds that I was to play over the next month. This was partially by design. The previous day at Tarbert was the first time I had even touched a club since that May 16 round at Sweetens Cove, when I had asked Jordan to play with me. A few days after the funeral, I received a handwritten note in the mail from a friend in Chicago. It ended with,

"When you are ready, you will find Jordan on the golf course. He will always be there with you."

I hoped that time alone on the course might help me process the unrelenting grief. The fact is, that since his death, I had not wanted to be around people at all. Always an outgoing person, I had been rigorously avoiding all human interaction. Being on the west coast of Scotland for a few days and talking to people—complete strangers in most cases—in the course of normal conversation had been a relief. On my first night in Lochgilphead, an old fisherman sat down next to me at The Comm Pub. Over our pints of Tennent's, we talked about fishing, US politics, the weather—thankfully anything other than what had consumed me since May 17. We would have gone on all night had Robbie not come in and announced my curfew. All the now painful memories and nightmares had left me isolated in a way I had never been before. Most days, I didn't know what to do. I was simply trying to make it from one day to the next. At this moment, it was nice to be standing by myself on the 1st tee of Isle of Seil Golf Club.

You can't see the ocean on the 1st hole, but you can smell it and sense that it's lurking around the corner, waiting for you. The wind coming off the sea is heavier somehow. Seagulls fly low over unimpressed sheep. Standing on the tee, Isle of Seil looks and feels like links golf. There's a certain hollow and resilient feel to the turf, along with the unmistakable scent in the seaside air. The opening hole at Isle of Seil is a surprisingly testing 406-yard par four. It plays to a large, gently rolling fairway that is shared with the 3rd hole, which returns in the opposite direction and crosses over the line of play for the 1st. The green is set in a nice corner of the property, against the backdrop of sheep and cattle grazing fields.

The 2nd tee is just a few steps from the 1st green. This 150-yard par three is completely blind, with the green situated on the other side of a steep hill. Trusting the small white aiming post, I sent an 8 iron in the general direction of the green. Cresting the hill, I smiled at the green site—complete with a few rabbit scrapes and set hard against an old stone wall. Sheep were grazing just beyond—blissfully oblivious to the golf. This small part of the course felt completely isolated. After holing out, I dropped a few balls on the gorse-enclosed plateau and hit chip shots for a few minutes. This perfect little hole is the type that you can only really find in Scotland. I walked over to the 3rd tee and solemnly rang the bell.

The 3rd tee sits on the same plateau as the 2nd green. The tee shot on this 403-yard par four is played down and across the 1st fairway. Preparing to hit my drive, I noticed a man in a red sweater on the extreme left side of the fairway, hitting balls toward the 3rd green. He appeared to be practicing wedge shots. The man looked back at me and waved. In my best American-visitor fashion, I hooked my drive straight at him.

"Sorry about that," apologizing as I walked toward the only other golfer on the course.

"No bother at all. I saw it the entire time. You stayed just out of the high stuff," as he pointed toward my ball. "My name is John. Nice to meet you. How are you getting on?"

Introducing myself, I said, "It's lovely so far. The turf is great."
"Aye, we do the best we can. It's not Muirfield. Four other members and I look after the course. We don't have a green-keeper just now."

"Well, I love it. This is my first time playing here."
I asked if there was anything to be done about the rabbits tearing up the fairways and greens.

"Aye, the rabbits. We used to shoot them, but the bunny huggers put a stop to it. Now the course is overrun. We may have to start shooting again," he said with a self-aware laugh.

We talked a few more minutes about the club, where he lived (nearby Isle of Luing), and my plans for the month. John Morgan proudly gave me the rundown on how to play the remaining holes of his beloved course. "Be sure to play from the wee back tee on the 6th, that's our 'Drive over the Atlantic,'" he said with a smile. Despite Covid paranoia and precautions, we shook hands. I was glad that we did.

"I would join you, but I just came out for a bit of practice before work," John said. "Off you go. Enjoy your game," he said, "I hope you'll come back again."

After the 3rd, holes 4 through 8 are located on the other side of the main road and play next to Balvicar Bay. They are all good, fun holes. The 4th is a beautiful 128-yard par three to a green located near an inlet from the bay, and it's surrounded by brilliantly colored native plants. On the 6th, I walked back to the semi-hidden, alternate tee—as John had advised—and hit the best drive of the day over the Atlantic. A bump-and-run 8-iron left me about 15 feet from the hole for birdie.

The course was empty as I stood on the edge of the 6th green and looked out over Balvicar Bay. Colorful sailboats waited patiently for their captains to arrive. It was a calm, peaceful scene. A man passed by on his morning stroll along the shore, his large black labrador dutifully following behind. The lab looked almost exactly like Champ, Jordan's dog and best friend for the last two years of his life. "Hello," the man said, "lovely morning to be out. It looks like you'll just beat the rain."

It struck me, as it had in the past, that people in this country are much more connected in their daily lives. They speak to each other and seem to have a genuine interest in the discussion. The seemingly mundane details of life—like the ever-changing weather or a 45-minute drive down the coast—are celebrated. In a refreshing way, these things take on a level of importance unheard of in the United States. As I watched them in the distance, the dog made a detour into the edge of the bay, before quickly rejoining his owner.

Buoyed by the man's smile and kind greeting, I made a conscious effort to think of a happy memory of my son. Jordan had been a beautiful putter and chipper. He could hit short game shots that would leave his playing partners laughing at the sheer outrageousness of the result. He could get up and in from anywhere—his high school golf teammates called this a "Jordan par." I recalled standing with his childhood best friend, Robbie Fields, on the 16th hole during the final day of the 2015 state championship. Robbie, now a college golf coach, had graduated a year earlier. When Jordan started playing on the high school team in 6th grade, Robbie would take him to practice and then bring him home. On the weekends, the two would hit balls together. They were inseparable for those four years. Robbie had come to Mobile, Alabama to watch Jordan and his former teammates try to win that elusive ring that he had wanted so much for himself.

We both sensed, as you always seemed to during high school playoff events, how close the ultimate outcome was. Every single shot was life and death. Jordan missed his approach shot well right of the green, not far from where we were standing.

'It's over, I said, he won't even be able to keep the ball on the green from there. It's impossible."

"He'll make a par," Robbie said, as if it was a foregone conclusion.

Jordan pulled out a wedge and took a full swing from a severe downhill lie. The green was impossibly fast and sloping sharply away from him. The ball flew straight up in the air and landed—in the only spot on the fringe that it could—and rolled out 10 feet past the hole. It was miraculous. "He'll make this putt, Jim," Robbie said calmly. His stroke was perfect and the ball never left the center of the cup. A few days after Jordan's death, I gave his friend that state championship trophy.

So far, my putting had been atrocious. The few pars I had made were the result of short, tap-in putts. I had no feel for how hard to hit the ball. As I studied the chance for birdie, I felt an unusual sense of calmness. I closed my eyes and recalled the beautiful, simple stroke my son had made that long ago day. My hands remained calm and the strike was solid. The yellow and black Callaway toppled in on the last roll. I heard "Good one, Dad" quietly, but clearly, in my mind. Tears started to roll down my face as I stared at the hole for several seconds.

Isle of Seil finishes with three consecutive par threes for a par of 31. The 155-yard 8th is a particular standout, playing over a tidal inlet of the bay. It's a beautiful hole. The 9th takes us back across Balvicar Road to complete the round. In fairness, it's the only pedestrian hole on the entire course. I finished and put my clubs away, half-hoping that John Morgan would still be around to talk some more. I was alone on the links. I went back into the golf shed and sat on the church pew for a minute. I felt this place deserved another moment of silence.

It was just another eight minutes down the single-track road to reach Ellenabeich, a beautiful, tiny village on the water with a store, café, and several houses. The small repetitive white buildings are the dwellings of former quarry workers, with just two rooms, each that originally contained a bed. An area that appears to be a harbor, and now serves as one, is actually the flooded remains of an old slate quarry. Towering over the small community is a sheer vertical cliff of exposed rock. It looks like a natural feature, but it's also a result of quarrying activities from the early 19th century.

The Easdale ferry captain was on his mid-day break, so I went into the Oyster Bar for lunch. As luck would have it, there was a table open, with an ocean view. Thinking it would be at least three hours before I'd be driving again, I ordered a pint to go with my cheese toastie and leek soup. I had an hour before the next ferry crossing. There was time to sit and reflect on the round. I remembered every hole at Isle of Seil vividly, even the unassuming 9th. This is the best sign of a good golf course.

Easdale—along with Luing, Belnahua, and Seil—is one of the Inner Hebridean Slate Islands. These islands are so rich in deposits of slate that in the 18th and 19th centuries, slate roofing became one of the biggest industries in Scotland. Slate from these islands was used on buildings all over the world. Many famous Scottish structures are roofed with slate from Easdale, including Cawdor Castle,

Castle Stalker, and Glasgow Cathedral. Slate production was halted in 1911, and the mining operation was abandoned. Today about 200 people live on this small, mile-wide island—accessible only by a small passenger ferry—inhabiting the dwellings of former slate company workers. The natural environment has slowly reclaimed the old industrial operations, giving the island a rugged, natural beauty. Island residents use brightly colored wheelbarrows—parked by the ferry landing—to carry their shopping to their houses. There's a strong feeling of sensitivity to the environment.

There was one person in line for the 1:30 ferry when I walked over to the landing. An older lady holding two shopping bags smiled at me and nodded. The ferry—really a small boat that seats about six people and their dogs—was empty and waiting for the captain to return. I felt a slight pang of guilt going out to visit this tiny island as a tourist, when people needed this boat just to get their groceries home. Thankfully no other passengers walked up before the captain invited us on. The tariff was £2.50 for a return ticket. I suddenly panicked, realizing I had no cash on me.

"Do you take a card?," I asked the somewhat imposing captain.

"Do I take a card? Aye. I prefer cards. This isn't 1950," he said, laughing. I liked him immediately.

The ferry crossing from Ellenabeich to Easdale takes no more than five minutes. At the landing, I noticed a group of colorful wheelbarrows. There are only unpaved footpaths on Easdale. The one tearoom on the island was closed due to the pandemic. For no particular reason, I started walking to the east. I heard the ferry start up and turned to watch it go. The small boat was framed by the backdrop of the massive rock formations of Ellenabeich. I felt momentarily jealous of the people who lived such a unique life on a tiny island in Scotland.

Robbie had advised me to take the time to walk all the way around the island. "You'll want to see where the old quarries have flooded with water," he'd said. It's no more than a 30-minute stroll. The views were stunning, as I followed the narrow, crushed-slate footpath past the small group of houses to the old quarry area.

Nature has a way of inexorably reclaiming the works of man. The old slate quarries were indeed beautiful, filled with clear blue water, and surrounded by multi-colored plants of purple, yellow, and red. I never even really thought about what the island used to be.

When I got back to the ferry landing, the boat was there waiting. A young couple with a white Labrador had already boarded. The dog looked at me expectantly. "Is it okay to pet him?," I asked.

"It's no bother," said the young lady. I rubbed the happy dog's head. Reaching into my pocket for my ticket, I couldn't find it anywhere.

Tapping and diving into my other pockets, I said to the ferry captain, "I can't seem to find my return ticket."

"I think we can make an exception just this once," he said with a laugh.

As the boat backed out of Easdale Harbour, I asked the captain if he enjoyed his work. "On this wee ferry? Aye. I get to meet new people every day. It's never boring. And look at my office," he replied with a gesture to the ocean. I could not argue with his logic.

5 IF I WIN THE LOTTERY

*"It is said that St. Columba and his disciples,
before they went to Iona in 563,
first landed in Scotland on the shore
at Southend."*

—Angus MacVicar, *Heather in My Ears*

Four days into this trip, I was beginning to enjoy life in Lochgilphead. When I returned from Ellenabeich, Robbie generously offered to drop me off for dinner at the Grey Gull Hotel in nearby Ardrishaig.

"You're on holiday, Jim. You should go out. It's no bother at all. Take your time and have a few pints if you like. I'll come pick you up when you're done," said my friend.

The dining room at the Grey Gull was open and airy, with large windows offering a view of Loch Gilp. Across the road, next to the loch, I could see a granite monument. While I was waiting for my table, I walked across the road to read the inscription. The tall, doric column, topped by a cross and an open bible, was dedicated to the memory of Reverend James Chalmers, a missionary to New Guinea. An Ardishaig native, he was murdered and eaten by cannibals in 1901, while attempting to spread the gospel. The sun was low on the horizon, and I could see the shinty pitch at Lochgilphead across the water. By the time I walked back to the hotel, my table for the evening was ready. After a couple of hours, enjoying my dinner and the evening immensely, I sent Robbie a text: "They have been playing A Flock of Seagulls and Modern English in the Grey Gull. I may be a little late tonight." He replied quickly with a laughing emoji. We were planning to make the 60-mile drive to Southend and Dunaverty Golf Club together in the morning. He picked me up in his small white car a few minutes later. It was for the best.

There's a palpable sense of history in the small village of Southend, some of it violent. In addition to St. Columba's first visit to Scotland, introducing the area to Christianity, Southend has a surprisingly rich and troubled past. The winding drive on the B842 from Stewarton stretches about eight miles through hills of exquisite rolling farmland, often with the sea in view beyond. Driving into town, you pass by Muneroy's Licensed Tea Room, and the lovely parish kirk—where renowned local author Angus MacVicar's father was minister for over 40 years. Aside from the golf course, Dunaverty Rock and the abandoned Keil Hotel are two of the biggest landmarks in Southend. I have never attended a service at the church, but I have visited Muneroy's several times over the years. As a long-time student of Scottish tea rooms, it's one of the best.

Dunaverty Rock, which is visible from almost the entire golf course, is one of the most historic spots in Scotland. It's believed that as early as 710 AD there was a fortification and castle located on top of the rock. Dunaverty Castle was once the center of authority for Clan MacDonald, who were known as the Lord of the Isles. This highly strategic location was fortified for almost 1,000 years. In 1306, King Robert the Bruce hid from enemy forces in the castle after instigating the rebellion against Edward I of England. Angus Og MacDonald of Islay helped him escape by boat, just before the

English laid siege to the clan stronghold.

The MacDonalds remained the Lord of the Isles and held Dunaverty Castle until the late 15th century. In 1494, James IV of Scotland took control of the castle. The Lordship of Kintyre and the castle was granted to Archibald Campbell, the 5th Earl of Argyll, in 1544. The bloodiest, and what proved to be the last and most infamous chapter of Dunaverty Castle, came in 1647. During the War of Three Kingdoms, part of the Royalist army force retreated here. Rival forces besieged the fortification and cut off the water supply. The trapped force of about 500 men eventually surrendered and were massacred at the base of Dunaverty Rock, at the direction of the Campbells. The castle was abandoned following the one-sided Battle of Dunaverty and was purposefully dismantled not long after.

Robbie and I were greeted warmly in the tidy Dunaverty club-house by Rona MacBrayne, who, along with her sister Ailie Goddard, is one of the club stewards. The sisters generally keep things running on a day-to-day basis at the club. Unfortunately, I had missed seeing them on my previous visit in 2019. We took some time to chat and catch up, as Ailie came in from the kitchen area to join the conversation. Rona took our lunch order, and we found a window seat with a view of the 1st tee and 18th green. It was 11am on a sunny Friday morning. A pair of older gentlemen were already finishing up their round on 18.

The current club captain—an ambulance driver from Campbeltown named Graeme—walked over, sat down next to our table, and introduced himself.

"It looks like you have a nice day to play," he said. "The course is playing fiery fast just now. I played in a competition last week, and one of my partners putted from 150 yards on the 13th. We've had quite a dry summer." We discussed how the club had fared through the Covid pandemic, since my last visit in 2019. "Our visitor play has been up, honestly," he said. As Rona was bringing our food, I asked if my recently published *Links Diary* story about Dunaverty had been well received at the club. I had always been somewhat nervous about calling too much attention to places as unique and special as this. "Yes, certainly. Everyone loves it," said Graeme.

"The only problem we have is people getting upset when there aren't any cows on the 1st fairway," said Rona cheerily. The cows, featured prominently in the wonderful photos for the story, only graze on the course for a few months of the year.

After our pleasant lunch conversation with Graeme, we went to the bar to settle our bill and make the short walk out to the 1st tee. Robbie still needed to pay his greens fee. "I'll sign him on as my guest," I told Rona proudly. It felt good to make full use of my Dunaverty membership, especially to help my friend save a few quid.

Visitors are treated with a level of respect in Scotland that is unmatched in the rest of the golf world. Since I had "signed on" Robbie as my guest, his greens fee for the day was only £10. Guests are considered a special thing at most Scottish golf clubs, much the opposite of the exclusive and often wildly expensive private club model in the United States.

Unlike the dramatic beginning to nearby Machrihanish, the charms of Dunaverty are not as readily offered. Beyond the clubhouse—and the warning sign for electrified fences—you see pleasantly rolling pastureland and the Irish Sea in the far distance. There are a couple of flags blowing in the wind. It's an unassuming view, yet there is a pervading sense that perhaps something special is to come.

Five holes at Dunaverty—1, 2, 3, 4, the 17 green, and 18—are located on the west side of Coniegien Water, a river that bisects the course on its way to the ocean. These holes are situated on land that the club leases from a local farmer who maintains grazing rights. The greens on this part of the property—as the sign forewarns—are surrounded by electric wire fences, which you have to step over to get to the putting surfaces. This isn't a concern in August, when the cows aren't grazing on the course. The club's lease with the farmer dictates that there can be no competitions on Sunday and no alcohol can be sold in the clubhouse. The parish church that Angus MacVicar's father once managed still holds some sway in this part of Scotland.

Dunaverty Golf Club was laid out by the original founding members in 1889. The routing has evolved over the years, but the current layout has remained largely unchanged since the 1930s. Like many great links courses, the first and last holes often serve to get the golfer away from the clubhouse and out to the best golfing ground. The 1st hole at Dunaverty follows this tradition. It's a straightforward uphill 301-yard par four, which should yield a birdie opportunity. The greens at Dunaverty are generally small and curiously rectangular in shape. They are also smooth and true, with stunning, jade-green turf.

After climbing the hill to the 1st green, the wondrous world of Dunaverty starts to reveal itself in earnest. The vast ocean, Dunaverty Rock, and even the northern coast of Ireland are all visible on a clear day. From this vantage point, the true nature of the linksland is exposed. Even after all the times I've played here, I am still stunned by the view.

One of the unwritten rules of remote Scottish golf is that there must be a caravan park located next to the course. The 2nd hole is a 157-yard, semi-blind par three, played toward a caravan park. Although it also lies in the less dramatic grazing land of the property, it's a fun hole and serves along with the 1st to ease the golfer into the round. During the walk past the caravan park to the 3rd tee, one of the great short par fours in golf, you slowly realize you are entering a golf dreamscape. At 279 yards, it's drivable, depending on the wind direction, yet the beach and Dunaverty Bay await any ball that drifts slightly right on the wind. It is a stunning hole—the first of many to come.

The 4th hole is a 162-yard par three called Dunaverty, due to its proximity to Dunaverty Rock. The tee shot is played completely blind over a large dune and down into a hidden dell, where a brilliantly situated punchbowl green awaits to gather a shot on the correct line. Angus MacVicar notes in the club's centenary history that the great James Braid himself suggested the current location for the 4th green. Braid had been visiting the area to consult on the design of The Machrie. You will play this hole with a smile on your face, if not outright laughing at its simple and unique perfection. Dunaverty has some of the most natural green sites of any links in Scotland.

One of the prized possessions in my golf library is a book I found in the old Quarto Bookshop in St. Andrews in 1994. It's titled *Golf in My Gallowses: Confessions of a Fairway Fanatic*, written by Angus MacVicar, a lifelong resident of Southend and member of Dunaverty Golf Club. He was an extremely prolific author, in both fiction and non-fiction, having written about 70 books, over 500 scripts for radio and television, and a few plays. Published in 1983, *Golf in My Gallowses* is a recollection of MacVicar's experiences in Scottish golf and playing at his beloved course, where he served as captain. Here he recalls a valuable lesson learned as a young man in the late 1930s, while playing the 4th hole with a much older Dunaverty member:

> The short 4th at Dunaverty is situated in a quiet hollow with tall, grass-covered sand dunes on three sides. Mr. Morton's tee-shot landed short, and it appeared to me that he would have to play a high pitch over the dune which hid the hole from him. When I saw him addressing the ball with a mid-iron and aiming almost at right angles to the direct line I wondered, in a moment of near-horror, if at last golf had driven him mad. Then his ball streaked through a small gap between the dune in front and the one on the left. It struck half-way along the downslope on the dune on the left, careered around the dry, close-cut grass on to the steep side of the dune behind the green and finally, like a toboggan on the Cresta Run, sped back and down toward the flag. It came to stop a yard from the hole. "Local knowledge," said Mr. Morton, patting my shoulder.

In the clubhouse, I had met 83-year-old Sandy Watson, a lifelong Dunaverty member. I asked if he had known Angus MacVicar.

"Oh, aye. I knew him quite well. He was a regular golfing partner of mine," he said.

"What was he like?," I asked.

"As a golfer? Or as a person?," he said, with a gleam in his eyes.

The holes from the 3rd through the 17th range from very good to great. At the 5th tee, the drive is over Coniegien Water (or River)—and off the farmer's grazing land—to continue a run of holes through the 11th that is my favorite stretch of links holes in the world. Before a second bridge was built over the river during course revisions in the 1930s, golfers used a small boat to ferry themselves across to the 5th fairway. Sandy Watson remembers his father talking about those days. "The holes on the Machribeg side of the river changed a lot over the years, up until after the war. On the Brunerican side, they have hardly changed since the beginning of the club," he told me.

At 257 yards, the 5th hole is a potentially drivable par four situated above Brunerican Beach. It's visually stunning and pure fun, as only a short par four on the ocean in Scotland can be. Playing in the same direction along the beach, the 6th hole, called Arthur's Seat, is an impossible, virtually unreachable, 245-yard par three. It's more difficult to make four on this par three than it is to make three on the previous par four. Yardage and par are irrelevant in Scotland. It's likely that a bogey on the 6th hole wins the honor as often as a birdie does on the 5th. Dunaverty is "only" 4,799 yards and a par of 66, but it does not need to be a single yard longer. It's both challenging and enjoyable, which is what a golf course should be.

The 7th and 8th continue the heavenly walk through this fantastic landscape. Both holes are great—especially the 392-yard 8th with its view toward Sanda Island—but they serve a higher purpose. They get us to the 9th, 10th, and 11th, which is one of the most transcendent three-hole sequences in golf. The 9th hole, Punch Bowl, is a 253-yard par four consisting of a blind drive over a massive dune, with a good tee shot careening wildly down the other side to yet another dramatic punchbowl green.

One of the great joys in golf is walking over a hill after a well-struck blind shot to see the result. As Robbie walked ahead, I paused for a moment at the top of the dune. I could almost hear Jake laughing out loud two years before, when he came over this hill—in the exact spot I was now standing—and saw that his drive was on the green. The ball was just sitting there in that natural bowl, with five feet left for an eagle two. At this moment, I would have given anything for him to be here with me. He had been a different person since his little brother died. All of us had. I worried about him, all the way on the other side of the world. You never cease to be a parent, even when your children grow up.

I had my own eagle putt today and received a quiet, "Well done, Jim" from my playing partner. Golf course architects cannot create something as good as the 9th hole at Dunaverty: only nature can.

The 123-yard 10th hole is called Mount Zion for good reason. It plays up a sheer, almost vertical hill to a large—by Dunaverty standards—plateau green that falls off precipitously on two sides. You could hit anything from a wedge to a 5 iron to this green, depending on the wind. Ascending to the promised land of Mount Zion, we are approaching the high point of Dunaverty Golf Club. For me, this has long been the spiritual summit of the entire golf world.

It's a short walk from the 10th green to the 11th tee. There's a bench by the red tee marker. I would normally sit down here for a few minutes, but today felt different. We were playing at a brisk pace, and I wanted to keep moving. I could sense that Robbie did too. This is one of the spots—along with places like the 9th tee at Cruden Bay, the 5th tee at Sweetens Cove in Tennessee, and the 17th green at the Old Course—that feels like the center of the golf universe. The drive on this 266-yard par four may be the single most enjoyable tee shot that many of us will ever hit. It takes us back down the steep hill that we have just climbed, both physically and spiritually. It is a good chance for birdie, or eagle if the wind is helping. The main challenge of the hole might, in fact, be the distracting views of the Mull of Kintyre and the Ulster coast beyond.

Moving inland and home toward the clubhouse, it will be hard to surpass what we have just experienced—but each hole is a delight. Leaving the seaside on the uphill 277-yard 12th, the proceedings become understandably more subdued—but only just slightly. The approach shot is played blind (once again) to a hidden green, with Brunerican Farm beyond. The 13th, called The Cemetery, is the only par five on the course and a particular standout among the inward holes. It plays wildly downhill, with a semi-blind approach to yet another wonderfully indigenous green site located at the base of massive dunes.

A 5,000-year-old standing stone sits just off the left side of the fairway. My ball has been magnetically attracted to the ancient monolith almost every time I've ever played the hole. Once again, I found myself walking down the left side of 13 in the direction of the Brunerican Stone, hoping I had stopped short of the dense bracken. Robbie, on the way to his normal spot in the middle of the fairway, called out, "Say hello to Claire and Jamie for me!" dipping into his endless supply of *Outlander* humor. It felt good to be walking and laughing.

The 17th, called the Burn, is the most well-known hole at Dunaverty. It's a strict par four of 412 yards that frequently plays straight into the prevailing wind. With the typical breeze, this is one of the most challenging holes in Scotland. The preferred approach shot is to play off the slope behind the green and let the ball roll back toward the hole. The rectangular putting surface lies hard by the devious river, which guards the green like Cerberus at the gates of Hell.

The water level of Coniegien Water varies greatly depending on the tides. It was high during our round, near the top of the banks. The wind was with us, dictating short irons into the green.

As Robbie was preparing to play, I remembered my dad hitting a career 3 iron onto the small, square green in 1994. I still have our scorecard from that round. We were both so happy that day, five years before Jordan was even born. Being at Dunaverty was such a wild and exciting adventure then: a father and son from Alabama in the hinterlands of Scotland. My dad had been completely devastated by his grandson's death. I thought about a photo that had been stuck on our refrigerator door for almost 10 years. It showed Jordan and my dad holding the junior club championship trophy at

Burningtree Country Club in Decatur, Alabama—the course that my father had played every Wednesday and Saturday with his regular golf buddies for almost 30 years. Most of those guys are gone now too. Jordan had become my dad's main golf partner as his friends slowly passed away. A flood of grief washed over me, but it passed quickly. Robbie had a great round going, and I didn't want to ruin it for him. This extraordinary golf hole had remained unchanged, but I was a completely different person now.

After crossing the insidious burn, the 17th green and the finishing hole are back in the farmer's land. It's a short climb to the elevated 18th tee. The 18th hole, a 323-yard par four called Machribeg (after the farm), is reminiscent of many closing holes in Scotland. Like the 18th at Prestwick or Fraserburgh, it mainly serves to get us back to the clubhouse as expeditiously as possible, generally on less interesting ground. My approach shot flew the green and went into some high rough. Robbie hit a lovely pitch to 10 feet and had a putt for a 64.

The sun never left us during this round, although it had gotten much lower on the horizon. A elderly couple was sitting on the patio outside the clubhouse, less than 30 feet away, enjoying a coffee. I chopped down on my ball with a 64-degree wedge and it flew toward the pin, bounced once, and hit the flag and fell in. The couple on the patio broke out into spontaneous applause, and I ceremoniously tipped my cap toward them. After our gallery settled down, Robbie calmly stroked in his birdie for a brilliant 64.

"That was well done," I told my friend as I shook his hand.

"Aye. Thanks for the game."

Ailie was finishing up for the day in the clubhouse and we stopped in to say our goodbyes. I promised to return to Dunaverty in a few days. Robbie drove us just down the road to see St. Columba's Footprints and the nearby cave where the holy monk allegedly spent his first night in Scotland in 563 AD. It was a remote and beautiful spot. Whether you are Christian, Muslim, or agnostic, it would be hard not to be moved by these surroundings.

We decided to drive over to the new Machrihanish clubhouse

for dinner. On the way, I asked Robbie to pull into the driveway of the old abandoned Keil Hotel as we passed by. The tall, imposing, white Art Deco structure seemed to tower over Dunaverty Bay. It was easy to stand there and think it was 1954, imagining a wealthy Glaswegian family was about to arrive any minute in a black Rolls-Royce for their weekend holiday.

"This place has always fascinated me. It must have been something to stay here in the 1950s," I said. "If I ever win the lottery, I'd buy this place and restore it."

"I'd join you, Jim," said my friend quietly.

6

CATRIONA MATTHEW'S CADDIE

"It is the garden of the game. Paradise, Elysium, El Dorado, and all scriptural and classical terms descriptive of happiness may be safely applied to East Lothian, and specifically the coast part thereof"
—John Kerr, *The Golf Book of East Lothian* (1896)

Lochgilphead at 5:30 am is eerily quiet. An older lady was already walking her dog and smiled at us as we carried our clubs across the street to the car. We had a 10 am tee time at Gullane No. 1, followed by a 3:20 afternoon time at North Berwick. The drive is roughly three hours across the country to East Lothian, a lengthy one by Scottish standards. Car trips that are viewed as a matter of course in the US are not undertaken lightly by Scots. Petrol is very expensive. Even some of the "A" roads require an extremely high level of unrelenting concentration. It can wear you out mentally. In a small country like Scotland, distances are perceived differently. Golf, however, is generally viewed as a somewhat valid reason for a long drive.

"We can stop in Dumbarton outside of Glasgow. There's a wee petrol station with good sausage rolls and coffee," said Robbie. My friend always considers the important factors first.

It had been over 20 years since I had last visited Gullane and North Berwick, two of the more well-known and historic Scottish links. In June 2000, I came to East Lothian with my dad, his brother Charles, and my cousin Chris. Charles and my dad were as close as brothers could possibly be. Charles was a golf nut, whose basement was so stocked with sets of new clubs that local golf shops would call him when trying to locate a special set of irons. He was a member of Shoal Creek and several other exclusive golf clubs but played the majority of his golf at Roebuck: a rough and tumble municipal course just outside of downtown Birmingham. Our families lived next door to each other for over 10 years. Consequently, Chris and I were more like brothers than cousins. Every summer, for almost 40 years, we all gathered on the Alabama Gulf Coast for a huge family holiday. Each day featured a round at a different local golf course, teeing off around 7 am, so we would be back before everyone could complain. Charles and I always played a straight up match against Chris and my dad.

Charles and Chris had both taken an interest in Jordan's golf. We had all played golf together many times, along with my dad. The five of us were playing together when Jordan made his first hole in one, when he was only 11 years old. My uncle gave Jordan his beloved Scotty Cameron putter, which had still been wrapped in plastic after 20 years. He had two brand-new models in his basement pro shop. Chris was the first person to come to our house the day Jordan died. He was one of the few people I could talk to that day.

We stayed at the Golf Inn in Gullane for several nights and played Muirfield, the three Gullane courses, North Berwick, Kilspindie, and a course called The Glen. One evening after a lovely long dinner at the hotel—and a few pints—we walked across the street with a wedge and a putter to play the wee children's course located in the middle of town. Along with St. Andrews, North Berwick, and Dornoch, it's one of the great golf villages in the entire world. A visiting golfer can stay in the 262-square-mile council area of East Lothian for an entire holiday and have quick access to more great golf courses than are available in most American states.

The Esso Lomondgate petrol station on the A82 at Dumbarton was busy with morning rush-hour traffic when we arrived around 7:30 am. Robbie went in to get a sausage roll while I filled the tank. You can still pump gas and pay inside the store in Scotland, a small perk of life that had disappeared over the last few years in the US. There was a large, red and green traffic light positioned over the entry doors. Fully masked customers could enter only when the light was green, thus keeping the number of people inside the store to six or fewer. In general, throughout this entire trip, it was evident the Scots handled the pandemic restrictions in a much more accepting and orderly fashion than I had ever seen at home the previous two years.

In his seminal book, *The Golf Courses of the British Isles* (1910), the great English writer Bernard Darwin wrote of Gullane:

> There is no other golfing centre that is quite so good as Gullane, in the East Lothian. If the golfer can only get up early enough in the morning, and has the strength to do it, he can play seven long courses on one long summer's day.

Gullane is a town given over to golf. The game has been played here for over 350 years. It's not unusual to see someone carrying a golf bag on the sidewalks of the quaint village, which has just the right number of shops and restaurants. The massive hill that shapes Gullane's topography is actually an ancient volcanic plug: the result of solid magma that cooled and formed hard rock inside a volcano that later blew into the Firth of Forth thousands of years ago. As Darwin rightly mentions, the options for golf in the area are almost limitless: North Berwick, The Glen, Winterfield, Dunbar, Kilspindie, Luffness, Muirfield, and Longniddry just to name a few. If you prefer to walk to your tee time, Gullane itself has three wonderful courses. Luffness and Muirfield are in Gullane as well.

We had been invited to play Gullane No. 1 by Harry MacLean, a former professional motocross driver who had retired from his sport to play golf and live in a house on Muirfield. Robbie had met him and a gentleman called Jeff Butcher who was also to join us, when the pair had visited Machrihanish earlier in the year. Harry and Jeff were frequent golf partners and played almost exclusively with hickory clubs. Jeff moved to East Lothian from his native England after being stunned on his first visit by the amount of truly great golf available in the area. Prior to our tee time that morning, the twosome had also graciously arranged a private visit for us with Boris Leitzow, the owner of Jack White's Golf Shop in Gullane.

Jack White's is a dream for lovers of golf history. We entered the shop a little after 9 am to find Boris waiting for us, dressed like James Braid in 1906. Hickory clubs and various items of golf memorabilia were crammed into every available inch of the small shop. An architect and native of Germany, Leitzow fell in love with the Gullane area and moved there after he purchased the golf shop in 2017. After our introductions, he handed Robbie a long iron from a set of clubs made by the legendary Tom Stewart of St. Andrews.

"You must feel the balance of these clubs. Just brilliant. Simply works of art," said our host.

Boris then embarked on a lecture on Scottish hickory club making that was as erudite as any scholar I've ever heard speak. I got the feeling this conversation could have carried on for hours—and I would have enjoyed it all—but Harry MacLean walked in to remind us of our pending tee time at Gullane. "We need to be on our way boys. The tee sheet is full today," said the imposing former motocross racer.

Gullane No. 1, where the legendary Babe Didrickson Zaharias won the British Ladies Amateur in 1947, is one of three courses in town: the others aptly named No. 2 and No. 3. When I first played here in 1997, the greens fees were very modest in comparison to the more well-known Scottish courses like nearby Muirfield. The European Tour brought the Scottish Open to Gullane in 2015 (and again in 2018), and the exposure and prestige of hosting this event—especially with popular American Rickie Fowler winning in 2015—has led to much higher visitor greens fees. Harry signed us on as his guests for the round—a very nice gesture on his part—saving us each well more than £100.

Our hosts treated us to a grand tour of the lovely members clubhouse, which had been expanded and renovated for the 2015 Scottish Open. A new, main entry highlighted many of the famous tour professionals that competed in the popular event. There's also a visitor's clubhouse, located across the A198 adjacent to the 18th green of the wonderful Gullane No. 3. The town revolves around the game of golf. We hit a few putts—Gullane has one of my favorite putting greens and opening tees in the world—and walked over to the Starter's hut. Knowing that we had a long 36-hole day ahead of us, I had asked Harry to arrange a caddie for the round.

Is there anything in life that offers the same sense of promise as the 1st tee of a golf course? The cloudless sky only added to the sense of anticipation. Robbie had never played Gullane No. 1, and his obvious excitement was contagious. The opening tee is a special place, situated as the epicenter of the golf-loving village. The sharply dressed starter and a tall, thin man in a royal blue caddie bib were waiting to greet us as we walked to the small hut.

"Lovely morning, is it not?," asked the guardian of the famous teeing ground.

We made introductions all around. Harry and Jeff were already well-known. Like Boris, Jeff dresses in the style of an early 20th-century golfer—think Harry Vardon. His attire and vintage hickory clubs must make him an easily recognizable figure around East Lothian.

Then we met our caddies. I shook the tall man's hand, and he said, "I'm Des. I'll be your man today." He took my bag, quickly removed a headcover, and handed me the driver. I liked him immediately.

The first seven holes on the No. 1 course play gradually around, and eventually up, Gullane Hill. The 1st is a perfect welcoming opening par four of 302 yards, and the 390-yard 2nd has one of my favorite approach shots on the links: a 7 or 8 iron played uphill to a beautifully sited green. Des and I began to talk in more detail as we walked down the 3rd fairway. It turns out he was a caddie on the European Tour for several years, most notably for the talented and much heralded Scot, Gordon Sherry. Sherry won the 1995 British Amateur at Hoylake, but his professional career never fulfilled the promise of his many amateur accomplishments. I asked Des why it never worked out for the talented Scotsman.

"Och, aye—I just don't know, Jim. He was a lovely player and could hit it for miles. Golf is a strange game. Nothing is guaranteed."

As we made the steep climb up the 5th and 6th holes and Gullane Hill, I started to notice the ongoing banter between my caddie Des and Jeff. Des was attempting to help Jeff with yardages and compliment him on seemingly good shots, but the Englishman was having none of it. "Nice strike!," Des would say enthusiastically, with Jeff replying, "No, no, that is absolute rubbish!" This went on for the entire round and left Robbie and I struggling to contain our laughter at times. Harry viewed this constant back and forth with a slightly bemused grin of a longtime golf partner.

The reward for the steep climb up Gullane Hill comes on the 7th tee, which is surely one of the great views in the entire sport. Muirfield, the Honourable Company of Edinburgh Golfers, lies below us in all its subtle and forthright glory. This scene is a reminder of how rare these vistas were before the proliferation of ubiquitous drone photos. To the left of the famous links—on the ground between the beach and the course—sits an area of natural dunes that looks like incredible golfing ground. I asked our hosts about the stunning natural dunes area.

"Yes, it's owned by the club. Jeff and I have walked around and hit balls in there a few times. It would be easily one of the great links, but I don't think it will ever be developed," Harry replied.

It seems Muirfield already has sufficient riches with its one great

Open championship course. Perhaps it's for the best that the area remains untouched for future golfers to dream about.

Gullane No. 1 is a lovely but strenuous walk. The par-four 11th, with the green situated so it appears to almost float in front of the sea beyond, is a particular standout for me. Fourball games are intended to finish in "3 HRS 45 MINS" at Gullane and—despite the constant verbal sparring between Jeff and Des—we made it right on the number. As we sat for a few minutes over our lunch in the lovely upstairs members dining area, I started to wonder if my legs would hold up for the afternoon round at North Berwick. I had not booked a caddie, and the thought of even pushing a trolley suddenly seemed to be a daunting task. I phoned the starter at North Berwick and asked if he could arrange someone to carry my bag.

"Well, it's unlikely seeing as you tee off in less than an hour, but I'll see what I can do," he replied nicely, but not encouragingly.

I was reluctant to end the brilliant conversation with Jeff, but it was time to leave. We said our goodbyes, with our hosts generously paying for lunch, and made the short 10-minute drive to the renowned West Links at North Berwick.

The town of North Berwick is like a smaller, less crowded, version of St. Andrews. Like Gullane, it's a town given over to golf. In the historic book, *The Golf Book of East Lothian* (1896), John Kerr writes:

> Everyone with an eye for the picturesque must be delighted with North Berwick. The town is rich in historical associations; fiction blends with fact to enliven the story of the past, as in the tradition that the devil once preached a sermon to a congregation of witches in the old kirk which stood near the present harbour. It is only, however, when we add golf to the attractions of North Berwick that we give it pre-eminence among watering places.

For those who don't study ancient golf literature, "watering places" is a Victorian euphemism for a health resort or holiday town by the sea.

The origin of the "West Links" at North Berwick (the "East

Links" is a wonderful headland course now called The Glen) dates as far back as the year 1790. The course has been the site of some of the most famous golf matches in history, including the infamous 1875 showdown between the Morris's of St. Andrews and the Park brothers of Musselburgh. In Stephen Proctor's excellent *Monarch of the Green,* on the life of Tommy Morris, he describes the magnitude of the match:

> Tommy and Margaret had barely settled into their new home when plans were announced for a foursome that would overshadow all the other golf played in 1875. In early September, after the autumn meeting at North Berwick, four titans of the game would face off. It would be Tommy and his father against Willie and Mungo Park, Open Champions all, for £25 a side.

The current layout developed naturally over time—most of the changes over the decades were implemented by the club members themselves—with some advice from Old Tom and others. In many ways, North Berwick, along with the Old Course and Prestwick, provides the original blueprint for golf course design.

I had played North Berwick many times before, but it had been almost 20 years since my last visit. As we walked toward the first tee to meet our host for the afternoon, the temperature suddenly dropped 10 degrees and rain began to pelt down. *Nobody in their right mind is going to come out and carry my bag in this weather on a Saturday afternoon,* I thought to myself. I somewhat timidly asked the starter if he had been able to find a caddie.

"Aye, I did indeed. He's walking up behind you just now."

A gentleman in a North Berwick caddie bib shook my hand, introduced himself as Graeme, took my bag, and walked over to the 1st tee. Robbie was already chatting with Joshua Ralston, our host for the afternoon.

It's safe to say that Josh Ralston is obsessed with North Berwick. A native Californian who moved his family to Scotland in 2015 to be a professor of Muslim Studies at the University of Edinburgh, he lived almost the exact life I had dreamed of trying to attempt 30 years before. He was on the waitlist for two years at North Berwick. As a member now, he plays most days that his teaching and family schedule will allow. I had corresponded with him for a few years, and we had narrowly missed playing together on a trip in May 2019. After talking for a few minutes on the first two holes of these ancient links, I was already getting lost in the wonderful conversation. It could quickly veer to a philosophical bent. Josh knew what had happened with Jordan and offered his sympathies before we reached this 2nd tee.

"I have no comprehension of the pain you must be feeling, Jim. I have children myself. I cannot even imagine what you are going through right now. Let's have a good time out here," he said kindly.

"I am going to try my best. I never know when it will hit me," I replied.

The years passed away as I remembered the previous trip here with my dad, uncle, and cousin. We had played our traditional Alabama match all over Scotland in that summer of 2000— always uncle/nephew versus uncle/nephew—and my dad had birdied the 18th to win 1 UP. These three had been my main golf partners for a large part of my life. In those younger days, I hated to lose. It was a tendency Jordan had as well, although he normally channeled it better than me. The memory of that trip now gave me comfort. We were all good players then, and I thought of how fortunate we had been to travel around Scotland together: the Old Course, Prestwick, even making it out to the Isle of Islay to play for three days at the Machrie. So many people put off doing things with their family—*I'll take my dad to St. Andrews one day, he's always wanted to go*—until it's the perfect time. But it's never the perfect time.

There will always be a multitude of reasons to put it off. You should do it now before it's too late.

I found that I remembered every hole clearly and felt a bit of regret that it had taken me so long to return to East Lothian. North Berwick is a living museum of golf. It has always been one of my favorite places. The skies suddenly cleared, and everything was now illuminated in a low, golden light. Walking toward the green on the great par three 4th, I asked Graeme how long he had caddied at North Berwick.

"Well, aye, for a while, off and on. I live right by the course. I've caddied on the European Women's Tour for about 20 years," he said.

"Oh, who have you caddied for?," I asked.

"Just one player: Catriona Matthew."

I suddenly realized who was caddying for me. As a golf nut, I knew that Catriona Matthew's husband was her longtime caddie. She is one of the all-time greatest Scottish golfers—the first Scottish female major champion—and the current Solheim Cup captain, with the matches just a few weeks away.

I exclaimed, "you're her husband!"

He smiled and said, "that's what I've been told."

The British & Irish Lions had a huge rugby test match on the tv that afternoon. Everyone had been talking about it for a few days. I asked, "what are you doing out here caddying for me on a Saturday afternoon with the rugby on?"

"I just enjoy meeting people and being out on the course. Almost without fail, I meet interesting people when I caddie here," he replied. We started to talk about his years on tour with Catriona. I asked Graeme what the highlights had been.

"Well, certainly the Solheim Cup captaincy this year has been very exciting. We are happy to be able to do it now with Covid ongoing. In general, there's nothing like the thrill of getting into contention, but I have to say that the victory at the Women's Open Championship at Lytham is the top moment for me. It was just a few weeks after our daughter Sophie was born. We had just narrowly escaped a fire in the place we stayed for the Evian Masters just before the Open. She was just trying to qualify for the Solheim Cup and wasn't really expecting to play well—then she won it. Sometimes when you are not expecting any results, you play your best golf."

Having played Royal Lytham & St. Anne's on a previous visit to the UK, I had always thought of it as the most underrated course in the Open rota. I was curious how Graeme regarded the elegant, historic links near Blackpool, England. "Lytham is simply brilliant. The bunkering is the best in the world. It's a thinking player's course," he said.

I was slowly tiring as we progressed rapidly around North Berwick. My legs were failing. The club allows for a much more generous time per round than Gullane—NO LONGER THAN 3 HRS 50 MINS—for a four-ball game. Robbie seemed to get stronger as the round went on, hitting one perfect, low-running draw after another. I apologized to Graeme for my increasingly poor play. "No bother at all, Jim. I heard your conversation with Josh about your son. I am so sorry for your loss, and I hope this takes your mind off things a bit," he said kindly. I briefly considered opening up to this nice man, but I was enjoying the day and our pleasant conversation. The thought of entering that universe of pain didn't seem appropriate.

There are so many good, if not outright famous holes on the West Links, but two have always stood out to me. The 14th hole is called Perfection, and rightfully so. In Patric Dickinson's sublimely poetic book, *A Round of Golf Courses* (1951), he writes of the hole, "Perhaps there ought to be a bit of luck in perfection, as beauty is enhanced by mystery and irregularity." Indeed, Perfection plays out like an exciting Victorian mystery. At 375 yards, long hitters can attempt to carry a ridge—with two cavernous bunkers—that bisects the fairway. Most normal players lay up short of the hill, leaving the approach shot played completely blind—and thrillingly downhill—to a green that sits majestically in front of the sea, like it's been there for 5,000 years. Somehow, I had managed a nice drive short of the ridge, and Graeme advised me to hit a pitching wedge, just right of the aiming pole. Once again, I made a solid strike and the ball finished on the front of the green, about 25 feet from the hole.

"Shot," said my overqualified caddie, as the ball flew away into the clouds. This is the highest praise a true Scottish caddie can, or will, ever give. After two putts for par on Perfection, my bad golf for most of the afternoon no longer mattered at all.

The other hole at North Berwick that's most special to me is the 16th, called Gate. It's similar in length to the 14th, at 378 yards.

The lush, back gardens of lovely Victorian homes and the imposing facade of the Marine Hotel are situated perilously close down the right-hand side—but it's the green on Gate that will long occupy a space in your golf dreams. It's similar to the Biarritz-style green that has been duplicated all over the world, most notably at the famous Chicago Golf Club, by Seth Raynor in a 1925 renovation of the original Charles Blair Macdonald design. Architectural historians believe that Macdonald (and his disciple Raynor) took their inspiration for the Biarritz template from a green located at a course in Biarritz, France. The source doesn't really matter, as the version at the West Links stands on its own merits. The long, narrow green, which drops off precipitously on both sides, is like a roller coaster. It climbs from the lowest level, through a deep, curving depression, to the top plateau. We spent several minutes hitting putts from the front to the far, back-hole location. Curiously, the green does not even rate a mention from either Darwin or Dickinson. According to club records, it was created in 1895 by the greenskeeper, Tom Anderson. It would be interesting to know what inspired him to create such a unique work of sculpture.

We all managed to make par on the wonderful 18th hole, which is like a first cousin to the last at the Old Course. Playing back into town is one of the great joys of many Scottish golf courses. I thanked Graeme once again for his service, but more importantly for the wonderful conversation, and I watched him walk off west toward home. Robbie contributed nicely to his tip, which is the proper thing to do when a single caddie is part of a larger game. We stood outside the clubhouse for a moment and thanked Josh for his generosity. He had refused to let us pay for our golf this afternoon.

"That was fun, Jim. I hope you'll come back and bring Jake," he said, as we put our clubs into the car boot. "There isn't much I can say. I hope being here has taken your mind off of things a bit." We promised to keep in touch. I was happy to have met Dr. Joshua Ralston—someone who had actually realized the dream I'd had 30 years earlier—a life in Scotland and a member at one of the great links of the world.

We sat in the car for a few minutes to collect ourselves, then started on the 15-minute drive back through Gullane to Aberlady. I had booked a room at The Ducks Inn for the night, in anticipation of an interesting evening with Robbie in Malcolm Duck's now famous golf bar. Thankfully, our rooms were on the ground floor. We managed to get situated for the night with relative ease. Malcolm had booked us a table in the dining room for 7:30. I told Robbie I would meet him there at the allotted time.

After sitting at our table in near silence for a few minutes, each slowly sipping a pint, it was obvious that we were both nearly overcome with exhaustion. Through the dining area into the bar we could see Malcolm Duck holding court. The nightly festivities were starting to get underway in earnest. It was going to be all we could do to order food and make it back to bed.

The food at Ducks is impeccable. A group of excited golfers, who had just arrived in Scotland for their first night of a week's golf, were ordering dinner at the table next to ours. I couldn't help but overhear the ongoing conversation. The first item listed on the menu under Main Course was "Seared duck breast with duck liver bonbon." All four of the gentlemen had agreed that they were going to order the duck.

The dining room and bar were packed, which I am sure is always the case at Ducks Inn during the height of the golf season. A young waitress came over to take the orders for the adjacent table of golfers.

"This will be easy for you. We will all have the seared duck breast," said one of the men.

"Sir, I am so sorry. We have just run out of the duck for tonight," the waitress replied apologetically.

In my state of physical and mental exhaustion, my normal filter wasn't in place. "Well, isn't that ironic ... at Ducks Inn, no less," I said so everyone could hear. Robbie and I nearly collapsed in a fit of laughter. It was good to be worn out from a day of golf.

7

PANMURE, THEN AND NOW

> "Tom Morris is believed to have contributed to the original Barry Links, close to Carnoustie and adjacent to Monifieth. However, reviews of the course led to Braid's invitation to lengthen the course in 1923."
>
> —John F. Moreton and Iain Cumming,
> *James Braid and His Four Hundred Golf Courses*

A full Scottish breakfast—eggs, sausage, bacon, tattie scones, black pudding, baked beans, mushrooms, tomatoes and toast, with a pot of tea—is one of the great joys in life. There's a lovely, reassuring, and welcome formality to breakfast in Scotland. I met Robbie downstairs in the dining room at Ducks Inn at 7 am, the first morning guests to arrive. We had nearly a two-hour drive ahead of us for our 11:30 tee time at Panmure Golf Club, just outside of the town of Carnoustie. A nice older lady took our order. I have never had a bad meal in Scotland when a nice, older lady has played a role in it. She brought us tea—and enough toast for 10 people—and put it on the table.

As she was walking away, Robbie asked, "Would you mind bringing us our toast please?"

The rack of toast she had just brought us was sitting right in front of him. I immediately started laughing, as the waitress just smiled. Robbie slowly realized his error.

"Aye, country comes to town," he said self-deprecatingly.

Panmure was largely designed by the great Scottish champion James Braid, whom according to English writer Horace Hutchinson, played golf with "divine fury." He won the Open Championship a remarkable five times. This is only one short of the record of six held by his contemporary and rival, Harry Vardon. Braid's victories came at the Old Course (twice), Muirfield (twice), and Prestwick. He was born in Elie in 1870 and learned the game there on its ethereal and elegant links. His most noted biographer, the legendary Bernard Darwin, wrote of Braid's 1908 Open win at Prestwick: "He dominated the tournament from beginning to end, serene, majestic, and inevitable."

After his celebrated playing career ended in 1928, Braid, the longtime professional at the famous Walton Heath Golf Club in England, focused even more on his second career as a golf course designer. From 1896 to 1950, Braid designed, remodeled, or modified over 400 golf courses in the United Kingdom. A partial list of his work in Scotland includes Brora, Golspie, Gleneagles (King's and Queen's), Stranraer, Reay, Boat of Garten, Ayr Belleisle, Lanark, Comrie, Fortrose and Rosemarkie, Muir of Ord, Rothesay, and Panmure. Almost without fail, his designs exhibit an elegance that reflects his upbringing at Elie and the even temperament so vividly described by Darwin. His courses appear to sit perfectly in the landscape and have a natural, almost calming, flow. They are similar, in that respect, to the work of another legendary Scot, and the first great golf course architect: Old Tom Morris.

I had first visited Panmure in the summer of 1994, on that memorable first trip to Scotland with my father. We stayed for two nights in a wonderful bed and breakfast on Links Parade, the street which runs adjacent to the 18th fairway at Carnoustie. After playing Carnoustie early one morning, we went across the street into the Caledonia Golf Club for a post-round drink. It's one of the local clubs associated with the legendary Open venue. I was recapping the highlights of our round (a three on The Spectacles for me!) with the bartender, who seemed genuinely interested in hearing our opinions of the course. At that time, the Open had not returned to Carnoustie since Tom Watson's maiden win in 1975 over an Australian, the great Jack Newton. The course had fallen a bit out of favor with the Royal & Ancient hierarchy in the 20 years since, but we had found it to be brilliant in every way.

Panmure was simply a name I knew from reading about Ben Hogan's historic 1953 Open Championship victory at Carnoustie, during his one and only visit to Scotland. I knew nothing about the course other than Hogan had thought highly of it and practiced there extensively in the run-up to the championship. The friendly bartender asked about our plans for the rest of the day.

"We don't have anything scheduled," I said. "Do you know much about Panmure?"

"Oh, aye, it's a cracking course. I'll call and see if you can get off this afternoon if you'd like."

Within five minutes he returned to our table with a tee time and, in those pre-Google Maps days of the '90s, detailed directions on how to find the course. It was a short drive and we had plenty of time to spare. We decided to have our lunch at the club, as we did almost every day on that trip. The directions were perfect—there were one or two tricky turns—and we drove down the long entry drive to find an almost empty car park. I can still remember that scene on a rare clear, sunny day: the stunning Victorian clubhouse, free-standing pro shop, and the ethereal greenish-brown, purple, and yellow links beyond. The architect in me was excited to visit the clubhouse, so we dropped off our bags by the pro shop and walked into the lovely wood-paneled bar to order lunch.

A well-dressed gentleman was standing behind the bar, which was completely empty. "We'd like to order lunch please," I said, trying as hard as possible to mitigate my Southern accent.

"I'm sorry, sir. The clubhouse is for members only," he replied sternly.

Suitably chastened and embarrassed, we quickly made our way back outside and decided to hit a few practice putts to kill some time. We had yet to see any other golfers, despite the perfect weather. Eventually we made our way into the pro shop to settle our greens fees. In those days, it must be said, the pro shop reception was perhaps even more icy than that of the clubhouse. Our greens fee was taken with very few words—I did not dare to even purchase a ball marker—and we were informed there was still 30 minutes before we were scheduled to play. The course was completely empty.

Thoroughly chastised once more, we stood outside the shop until our appointed tee time. In all fairness, the club had allowed us to play on very short notice. Imagine a bartender in Southampton, New York calling National Golf Links of America to see if two guys from Alabama could play that afternoon. However, the total lack of welcome was a bit shocking to the senses. In all my years of visiting Scotland, it remains an almost singular occurrence. Thankfully, the brilliance of the links overcame our sensitive feelings. We had it all to ourselves.

After three pleasant but somewhat prosaic opening holes, Panmure entered the realm of the fantastic. It was a landscape of almost bizarre linksland, with a heathland feel, all framed by ever-present, vividly purple heather. Shot after shot was fun and strategic. I remember my dad laughing several times as we stood on a tee trying to determine the best line over the moonscape of dunes and natural mounds. We finished, avoiding the pro shop, and drove back to have our post-round drink at Caledonia Golf Club.

I must admit, although I loved everything about the golf course, the experience kept me from returning for over 25 years. It was my loss. It was 2021, and a lot had changed. It was time to see Panmure again. But first, Carnoustie.

It was a Sunday morning and the drive up from Aberlady to Carnoustie was an easy one. I had somehow managed to get the rented Toyota through the impossibly narrow 1800s-era arched carriageway at the Ducks Inn without a scratch. We arrived in Carnoustie earlier than expected, so we decided to visit the historic links and look around. The Women's British Open was scheduled to be held there in fewer than two weeks. There wasn't a cloud in the sky as we sat down on the veranda outside the "new" hotel overlooking the iconic 18th green. It had replaced the old, concrete-bunker style clubhouse that had been the backdrop to that memorable finish in 1975. A cappuccino, a flat white, and some biscuits were soon brought to our table. The massive Open grandstands were in place. It would be hard to imagine a more peaceful golfing scene.

While sipping our drinks in silent reverie, no golfers had come up the 18th. I told Robbie that I wanted to walk out to where Jean van de Velde had lost the 1999 Open—with his inexplicable third shot—only needing a double-bogey six to win the Claret Jug. Nobody stopped us as we walked around the green. I had forgotten how close the out-of-bounds fence sits on the left-hand side. The course was immaculate, as good as I have ever seen. We stood on the bridge over the famous Barry Burn and took it all in—the grandstands, the hotel towering above, the bright yellow scoreboard—without saying a word.

Following this moment of silent respect, we walked over into the spot in the rough where the mercurial Frenchman gave away the most famous trophy in golf. The fescue rough was high, but wispy. You could almost imagine how van de Velde thought he could pitch it over the burn and onto the green, instead of sideways into the fairway—and almost certain victory. Maybe when everything has gone right for you, that's the moment you can't imagine something going wrong.

"I guess it all depends on the lie, Robbie."

"Aye, it's tempting. You can see how it might've happened."

We had been invited to play Panmure by Glasgow native Kenny Pallas, one of the co-founders (along with fellow Scots Jamie Darling, Stu Currie, and Graeme McCubbin) of *The Links Diary*, a brilliant new Scottish golf journal started in 2020. I had written stories for the first three issues and was excited to finally meet Kenny in person. He had made a brief attempt to play professional golf before realizing, like most people do, that it's a nearly impossible challenge. His love for the game was now channeled into *The Links Diary*, which celebrates everything that is unique and special about golf in Scotland. After Jordan's death, Kenny and Jamie were among the first to reach out to me. They sent a lovely video tribute that I played for our family on the horrific morning of his funeral. In the face of such an unthinkable situation, people have no idea what to say. Over beautiful video footage of Dunaverty, the following words from an ancient Celtic prayer slowly appeared:

> May the road rise up to meet you.
> May the wind always be at your back.
> May the sun shine warm upon your face;
> May the rains fall soft upon your
> fields, and until we meet again,
> May God hold you in the palm of His hand.
>
> In Memory of Jordan Hartsell

It was a small, thoughtful gesture that somehow gave us all—especially my poor dad—a bit of comfort.

The drive from Carnoustie to Barry is 10 minutes at most. When we arrived, everything appeared unchanged from 1994—except for one critical thing. We were greeted in the perfectly stocked pro shop like we were members of the Royal & Ancient Golf Club. We were made to feel as welcome as any place I'd ever visited. The friendly professional and his assistant encouraged us to visit the clubhouse for lunch or a post-round drink. The change in attitudes over 25 years was so different that I mentioned it to Kenny on the first tee.

"Aye, I've heard it used to be that way. To attract younger mem--

bers, I think the club needed to change. Our secretary is great and has gotten the club onto Instagram and Twitter. Visitors are really encouraged to come here now," said our host.

Thankfully, the brilliant design of James Braid, so beloved by Hogan, remains the same. The years rolled away as we walked quickly down the first fairway. I thought of that long-ago round with my dad. Every day in Scotland had been like a dream to us.

Panmure is a course that you could play every day and never grow tired of. It's endlessly fascinating. Final qualifying for the nearby Women's Open was to be held the following day and—like its more famous neighbor—the conditions were near perfect. Several of the young pros were out playing, or just walking, the course with caddies or family members. We spoke to many of them as we made our way around. The popular American professional Christina Kim was playing a few holes behind us. It was a perfect day to be out on the links.

Despite the passage of time, I found that I could recall almost every hole. At the beautiful 402-yard par-four 4th, after a walk through a lovely stand of Scots pines, the tumbling, enigmatic linksland of Panmure begins in earnest. You play hole after hole here with "pleasurable excitement," to once more quote the great Darwin. The 144-yard par-three 5th hole is called Punchbowl, and it plays over turbulent, rough linksland to a brilliant, multi-tiered semi-punchbowl green. It's pure fun. Short par-three holes remain thankfully abundant in Scotland, even if modern-day designers have all but abandoned it for inexorable, 230-yard monstrosities.

Unsurprisingly, the 6th hole is called Hogan. The "wee ice mon" said it was one of the best par fours he ever played. A devious greenside bunker was even added at the great man's suggestion. It's a perfect strategic hole. Standing on the tee, it's a puzzle. The more direct line offers a shorter approach, but the shot is blind. A tee shot played to the right side of the fairway offers a clear view of the green, but a longer approach and a less-favorable angle. The green sits exposed on top of a dune framed by beautifully devious heather. This is Braid at his finest. Kenny's excitement was palpable as he described how much he loved the hole. It's soon followed by the 361-yard par-four 8th, called Dunes. The tee shot here lures the golfer to playing out to the right, when the correct line is much farther left than you would ever comprehend. The green is perfectly sited and allows for a variety of fun approach shots. It is one of my favorite holes in the world.

When we reached the par-four 12th, with the impossibly snaking Buddon Burn winding its way between the end of the fairway and the exposed tabletop green, I could no longer contain my outright joy of being back at Panmure.

As we watched one of the young professionals play down the 13th, I said, "I had forgotten how incredible this place is, Kenny. I'm sad it's been 25 years for me. Thank you so much for inviting us today."

Robbie echoed my sentiments. He was playing well, as is his custom, and clearly enjoying his first trip to the Barry links. We had been laughing and joking all the way around.

As we turned toward home, the gently waving fescue, fields of violet heather, the occasional Scots pine and the ScotRail train speeding toward Dundee perfectly accented every elegant, poetic, and subtly strategic hole. On 18, I purposefully stayed several feet behind Kenny and Robbie in order to get a photo of them walking together. The brilliant white clubhouse shone like an ancient Greek temple in the sun beyond. Once more making up for (and surpassing) the lack of welcome in 1994, we had a lovely late lunch on the patio outside the member's bar. Panmure—such a charming, elegant James Braid design—was completely redeemed for me.

Robbie and I had a long cross-country drive back to his home in Lochgilphead ahead of us. Kenny walked with us out to the car park to say goodbye. Kenny embraced me and said, "thanks for everything you've done for *The Links Diary*, Jim. I hope being here for a few days has helped you some, my friend." Whenever I would start to feel the emotion and pain return, it would come quickly and sharply. A series of moments, if not years, could flash through my mind in the matter of seconds. I remembered how proud Jordan was when he read my stories in the first two editions of *The Links Diary* on Cullen and Dunaverty.

On those occasions, we had talked about golf the way we used to do when he was younger. "There are really cows on the golf course at Dunaverty?," he asked me with a laugh. He was a huge fan of Todd Schuster and Phil Landes of No Laying Up—who I had interviewed for the Cullen story—and wanted to know everything about the course. He had watched their YouTube *Tourist Sauce* videos from their Scotland trip. Jake and I had played with George Clark, who appears in one of the NLU episodes, at Cullen in 2019. "Was he fun to play with, Dad?," Jordan wanted to know. The last time I saw Jordan mowing the green that he had built in our backyard, he was wearing a No Laying Up tee-shirt. It had their familiar "fore left" logo emblazoned on the front. He had taken the shirt from my office without even asking, not that I had cared.

"Yes, Kenny, it has," I replied, choking back tears, "Thanks for everything you guys have done since it happened. It has meant more to me than you will ever know." Those first two issues of Kenny's wonderful journal had given me a few good moments with Jordan, in a time when he was largely withdrawn from us. On the back cover of *The Links Diary* issue #3, the editors printed a dedication: *In Memory of Jordan Hartsell*.

Over the last few holes of our round, I had silently dreaded the upcoming drive. But a day of golf, with two fine people, at Panmure seemed to give me some renewed energy. The trip was a pleasure, and the conversation never stopped. Along the way, Robbie excitedly pointed out course after course—St Fillans, Comrie, Killin—that I made a mental note to play later in the trip. When we finally parked in front of Robbie's house, the neighborhood was dead silent in the yellow-gray twilight. Foregoing the welcome promise of bed, we sat in his den and watched the golf from America. I don't think either of us wanted the day to end.

The Shore Hole at Shiskine (photo by Hamish Bannantyne)

Jordan (center) and his HHS teammates after a victory

All photographs by author, unless otherwise noted

The 8th at Cruden Bay (photo by Kaylin Quinlivan)

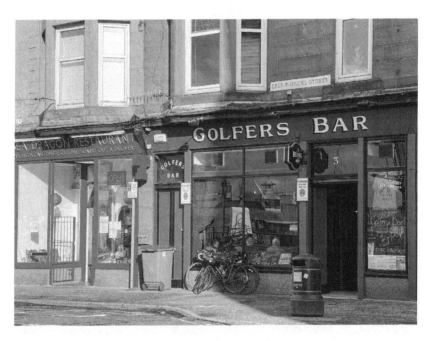

The Golfers Bar in Rothesay on the Isle of Bute

Isle of Colonsay Golf Club

The Sea Captain's House at Dunaverty Rock

JIM HARTSELL

The 6th at Durness

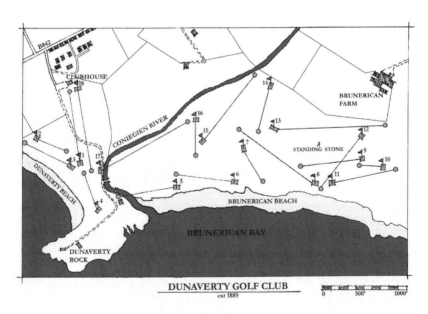

Current layout of Dunaverty (drawing by author)

Jake on the 13th at Cullen in 2019 (photo by Kaylin Quinlivan)

Dad at Machrihanish, 1994

The 1st at Brora

The 13th hole at North Berwick

The 2nd green at Dunaverty

The 1st at Isle of Skye

JIM HARTSELL

The 7th green at Gairloch

The 2nd green at Bute

Robbie Wilson in Kilmartin Glen (photo by Tom Shaw)

The Mannie, looking over the 14th at Golspie

Reay

The 2nd at Corrie on the Isle of Arran

Chris McBride and the author on the Alps at Prestwick

Harry MacLean in trouble on the 12th at Machrihanish,
as his partner Jeff Butcher looks on

The abandoned Keil Hotel in Southend

Dunaverty, from the 5th tee looking toward the clubhouse

The 7th at Shiskine

The Bridge over the Atlantic

JIM HARTSELL

The Isle of Seil clubhouse

Hogan's hole at Panmure

Open for play at Durness

The 9th at Brora

JIM HARTSELL

Mt. Zion at Dunaverty

Jordan

INTERLUDE
FATHERS AND SONS

"Life separates us too soon. That's what my father had said on the road to Scotland."

—James Dodson, *Final Rounds*

As far back as I can remember, I was spending time at the golf course with my dad. When I was a small child, every weekend we would go to Trammell's Driving Range and Par 3, on Highway 11 near Trussville, Alabama. It wasn't unusual for us to also go one night during the week, too. The par-three course was illuminated with large flood lights, so we could play until 10 pm. It's a Target shopping center now. The world is a lesser place because of it.

When I became old enough, my dad would take me to Roebuck, our local municipal course. That was where he had learned to play golf with his brother. Sometimes if we were lucky, someone he knew through work might invite us to play at the Country Club of Birmingham. Thinking back on it now, that must have been such a big deal for him, yet he always got me included in those rare invitations: a nine- or ten-year-old kid who could only hit it 150 yards.

During those years, I also had a normal Sunday game with my grandfather at Roebuck. It was just the two of us. He would pick me up at our house in Tarrant City as soon as we got home from church. Our tee time varied, depending on how long the preacher at Rock Methodist had threatened us with the fires of Hell. As my late grandmother would say, the reverend was "kindly long-winded." I often played the first five holes at Roebuck in my head, shot by shot, as the interminable sermons wore on. My grandfather and I always played 18 holes on those Sunday afternoons. Without fail, we went to one of his favorite restaurants on 1st Avenue North in Birmingham after the round. He had been involved in heavy fighting in Europe during World War II. He never talked about it. I like to think that all those years of golf were his reward for the horrors he must have seen in France and Italy. He played with clubs from the 1940s. I still have a few of them in my office.

Around the age of 12, I started to take golf even more seriously. I'd hit plastic balls for hours on the course I had created in our backyard. Three different balls would be in play: one would be Jack Nicklaus, one Arnold Palmer, and the third Tom Watson, or sometimes Seve Ballesteros. The hole would always be played for the Claret Jug. All putts had to be holed out, just like a real tournament. I raked the dirt green every day to keep it smooth. To this day, I can putt serviceably on dirt with an 8 iron. The backyard Open Championships were strictly a one-club affair.

Around this same time, my dad was able to join a modest private golf club located about 30 miles north of Birmingham, called Cumberland Lake Country Club. Until I was 17, we played there every Saturday. It was a tough layout, located in the lovely foothills of the Appalachian Mountains. We always walked, no matter how hot it was. My dad did not believe in golf carts. In the summer, he would drop me off at Cumberland at 7:30 am and pick me up at dark. When I became a father, I wanted my boys to have the same exposure to the game I loved.

Jonathan and Jake are less than two years apart in age. They were inseparable when they were little. I started taking Jonathan to the driving range when he was about five years old. Before too long, we had no choice but to take Jake with us. They'd hit balls—or attempt to hit balls—until they were worn out. On the shelf in my office, right next to golf balls from places all over Scotland, I have an old Titleist from Jonathan's first birdie, when he was seven years old. I still remember how happy he was when he made that putt. You would have thought we both won the lottery

Any golf-loving parent out there knows that there are a lot of other sports that compete for your kids' attention. Jonathan eventually started gravitating to baseball and football. Jake stuck with golf longer, winning the Morgan County Junior Championship when he was 12. He had a lovely, repeating swing and a beautiful touch around the greens. One of the best natural athletes I've been around, he was also a great baseball and basketball player. Those were the sports he ultimately chose to focus on. It makes me happy that they both love golf today and play whenever they can.

Jordan was different. He was obsessed with golf from the first time I took him to hit balls on the range. At age two, he could hit a plastic ball all the way across our yard with a short, quick swing. He was also a great baseball player in a baseball-obsessed small town. When he was almost 11 years old, he asked me if it was okay to quit baseball and just focus on golf. I could not have been more thrilled. I immediately got him a junior membership at Burningtree, our local golf club. It was only $100 a month, and he would practice and play endlessly. Like my father had done 25 years before, in the summer I'd drop Jordan off in the morning and pick him up at night. It didn't matter to me if he charged three cheeseburgers a day on his account. I never said a word and paid the monthly bill happily.

As he got older and started driving, he still spent most of his time at Burningtree. He dearly loved that golf course and some of his friends there. It made me happy that he was carrying on the tradition of golf in our family. He was something different though: a real talent. On the weekends when I knew he was practicing late in the day, I'd drive out to Burningtree and watch him hit balls. I would sit quietly in a lawn chair several feet away. Occasionally, he would ask what I thought about a particular swing or shot that he was working on, but only rarely.

One breezy spring afternoon, he asked me the best way to play a punch shot in the wind. He knew how much I had played in Scotland, so maybe I knew something useful on this one topic. I took an 8 iron and showed him how it was done at Dunaverty and Machrihanish. Within minutes, he was striking low, rising 8 irons into the setting sun. This was as close as we ever got to playing in Scotland together.

For many years, I was his caddie and business manager. I made sure he was entered in tournaments and always drove him to the events, sometimes leaving at 2 am to make an 8 am tee time. The night before each tournament, I would clean his clubs with a toothbrush. I made sure he had plenty of high number Titleist balls, the kind that he always played. I loved every minute of it. Around the start of his last year of high school, my golf responsibilities started to curtail. Then, magically, he asked me to caddie for him again several times in the summer of 2019. He had decided to give college golf another try, and he was suddenly himself again. After we finished one round in a USGA qualifier that summer, he said, "you are a really good caddie, Dad." It's one of the best things anyone has ever said to me.

Golf is a way for fathers and sons to communicate, even more as they get older. My dad is 78 now and still talks about our trips to Scotland decades ago. He can still tell you what club he hit off the beach on the 1st hole at Machrihanish or about the time we both made birdie on the 15th at Cruden Bay. We still talk about walking up the 18th hole at the Old Course in the long shadows on a late afternoon in August. My boys text me nonstop during the final round of PGA Tour events, if they aren't out playing somewhere. We constantly speculate on future golf trips together. I may not hear from Jake for several days, then out of the blue, I'll get a text message that says something like, "Anstruther is my favorite golf course."

It has often been written that baseball is the language of fathers and sons. For our family, it has always been golf. You can't play baseball with your dad when he is 78, but you can get in nine holes with him on a cool, Fall Saturday morning. If you're lucky, your sons—his grandsons—will be with you. And if you're lucky again, it'll be you out there with your sons and grandsons in your later days. On the way home, you can all stop at his favorite barbeque place, which is your favorite one, too.

Golf is often a game for fathers and sons, but it's more than a game. It helps us communicate; it helps us relate. That's how it's been in my family for generations. And that's the only reason why—after a necessary break—I returned to golf after Jordan's death: I keep playing in the hope of finding my lost boy.

8

THERE WILL BE NOTHING TO BE DONE FOR YOU

"The machair of Colonsay is so smooth that golf was once played on it."
—John McPhee, *The Crofter and the Laird* (1970)

Robbie had an important meeting with his bosses from Glasgow the morning after our return from Panmure. The day was mine to spend alone, so I decided to take an unhurried drive back down the A83—stopping for breakfast by Tarbert Harbour—and play an afternoon round at Dunaverty. The weather forecast was meant to be perfect—yet it was dark and rainy as I left Tarbert and continued on through Clachan, Tayinloan, and Bellochantuy. At Tayinloan, no more than a small collection of well-kept houses, I saw the sign for the short ferry crossing to the Isle of Gigha.

There's a nine-hole course there that has always intrigued me. I briefly considered taking the ferry across but kept going. The ruins of an old, medieval chapel appeared on my right. Its wooden roof structure was long gone, but the stone-buttressed walls remained—a lasting testament to the skill of some ancient Scottish craftsman. Not far outside of Campbeltown, on the road to Machrihanish, is the Stewarton turnoff for Dunaverty. Even after so many years, I still felt a small thrill of excitement as I made the turn south.

After a few minutes, just as I passed a small sign for the Mull of Kintyre, the skies magically cleared, and the sun broke through. My dad and I had walked down to the lighthouse all those years ago in 1994. He had wanted to see the coast of Ireland, just 12 miles from the famous point. Angus MacVicar's parish church was bathed in a surreal golden light as I entered the small village of Southend. The windows on the stone narthex shone brightly in the sunlight below the simple, gabled, end wall of the sanctuary. On the left, the old Argyll Arms Hotel was closed: perhaps another casualty of the global pandemic. At one time, it was the main gathering place for Dunaverty members to have their post-round dram of whisky, since the owner of Machribeg Farm forbade the serving of alcohol on his property. This restriction continues to this day. At the sign for Teapot Lane, the art deco storefront of Muneroy Licensed Tea Room & Store appeared like an old friend.

I was greeted warmly by Ailie Goddard, who runs the Dunaverty clubhouse with her sister Rona. On my prior visit in 2019, I had just missed seeing her, so we talked for a few minutes about all the happenings at the club. I ordered lunch and took a seat by the windows looking out to the 18th green. A threesome of elderly gentlemen was just finishing their morning game.

"You've pretty much got the course to yourself this afternoon, Jim," said Ailie as she dropped off my (always perfect) ham and cheese toastie. "There were a few that went off quite early, but they're all finished now, but one or two groups."

I noticed an older gentleman enter the dining area. He quickly ordered lunch and took the table next to mine. We were the only two people in the clubhouse, other than Ailie. As soon as he sat down, he turned and introduced himself as Jim Gubler from Nevada. The name seemed vaguely familiar to me.

When I replied that I was from Alabama, he said, "What's an American doing at Dunaverty?"

"I could ask the same of you," I replied with a laugh.

My new friend went on to tell me that he was a retired judge and owned a house in Campbeltown. "I wrote a book called *A Golf Lesson at Machrihanish*," he said proudly. Then I remembered where I had heard the name. As an obsessive collector of books on Scottish golf— even the most obscure—I had read his novel a few years earlier. My main recollection of the story was an attempt to write in Scottish dialect, which I did not think had been very effective. A friend in Campbeltown, Hugh Sinclair, had originally told me about the book. He mentioned that it was a thinly veiled story about actual people in the area, with fictional names, and had annoyed a few locals when it came out. I replied that I had a book coming out myself—and also wrote for *The Golfer's Journal* and *The Links Diary*, neither of which he had clearly ever heard of. "Enjoy your lunch. It was very nice to meet you," I said as I walked out to the 1st tee. Ailie smiled at me somewhat sympathetically.

I had a peaceful, deliberate walk around the empty links of Dunaverty. At the 9th, the brilliant, blind 253-yard par four called Punchbowl, I took a sequence of photos from the tee to the green. When I reached the 11th tee, I sat on my favorite bench and texted the photos to a friend, Rob Collins—a great, up-and-coming golf course architect. His passion for fun, quirky holes is equal to mine. The response was almost immediate: "Wow! That's incredible. What a hole." I walked back to the medal tee on Mount Zion and looked out at the yellow-green fields of Brunerican Farm. The tall fescue was rolling in the wind like waves of the nearby sea. It was like a scene from a Terrence Malick film.

When I walked off the 18th, Ailie was in the car park about to leave for the day.

"That's you then?," she asked cheerily.

"That's me. I think I'll go for tea at Muneroys."

Scottish tea rooms are often the social hub of small communities like Southend, Machrie Bay, or Corrie. They are a place to sit with a small, restorative pot of tea—maybe have an impromptu conversation about the weather or the local golf course—and perhaps even a piece of cake. Muneroy's Tea Room is full of memories for me. My dad and I had stopped there on our first visit to Dunaverty looking for a Coke and wound up staying for an hour. Frances, the owner and pastry chef, makes cakes and desserts that defy logical description. People come from all over Argyll for their afternoon tea at Muneroy's—or to get a piece of takeaway pastry. I ordered tea and chocolate sponge cake. A table of ladies next to me were having a birthday party. They asked me to take their photo. For a moment, I felt envious of the happy group of friends. Birthdays and holidays have always been major events in our family. I couldn't even comprehend having another Thanksgiving, Christmas, or birthday celebration without Jordan. It was difficult to be sad in a place like Muneroy's, so I took the photo while trying to put a smile on my face.

We were booked on the CalMac ferry from Oban to Colonsay early the next morning and I needed to start back north to Lochgilphead. Passing glorious Westport Beach, one of Robbie's favorite spots, I decided to pull over into the empty car park. The beach is often frequented by surfers. The waves were pounding as I walked to the edge of the vast Atlantic. I took off my shoes and turned back to look for Paul and Linda McCartney's High Park Farm, in the distance on the hill overlooking the strand. The hillside was dotted with sheep. It was obvious why the famous Beatle had felt at peace with his family here for so many years.

Alone on the sand, a vivid flashback passed through my mind: of Jordan at three or four years old, running through the Alabama surf in a fit of laughter. His two protective older brothers were not far behind, should anything go wrong. It seemed impossible and ridiculous that this perfect, happy boy was gone: that my perfect, happy family was destroyed. For the first time all day, a wave of undiluted grief washed over me, stronger than the constant waves of Westport

Beach. I almost collapsed. After a few seconds, the moment slowly receded. I walked back through the sand to the car park. A young couple were getting out of a camper van with two excited golden retrievers. The happy dogs seemed to bring me all the way back to the present. An hour later, I was back in Lochgilphead picking up some takeaway Chinese food for Robbie and I.

The lovely seaside town of Oban is only 37 miles from Lochgilphead. For an American driver, the trek up the beautiful and impossibly winding A816 takes at least an hour. The speed limit is 60 mph, but 45 mph on this road feels as if the upper limits of safety are being challenged. The drive through Kilmartin Glen and past the lochs of Craignish and Melfort is a tour of ancient Scottish history. Robbie pointed out some of his historic sites that we had not been able to visit a few days earlier—ancient hill forts, cairns, and standing stones seemed to be around every curve. We stopped briefly at the site of Dunadd Hill Fort. The ancient stronghold was once located on top of a rocky hill that rises dramatically above Moine Mhòr, a vast bog at the southern end of the glen. It was the seat of power for the Gaelic kings at the very beginnings of Scotland. A footprint carved into the rock near the top of the hill is called the Kingship Stone, thought to be the spot where each new king made a vow to serve the people of the glen. Robbie proudly showed me a cast metal sign that he had lovingly restored. The ferry check-in was at 8:30, and we had given ourselves plenty of time for the trip. Traffic was light at such an early hour.

Oban is the largest city on the west coast. It's a wonderful old seaside town filled with families enjoying the waterfront and the many fresh seafood shops and restaurants. It's also the location of a major ferry terminal with sailings to the islands of Mull, Coll, Tiree, Barra, South Uist, and Islay. There was only a single sailing, five days a week, to Scalasaig on the small, remote island of Colonsay. We parked in the gathering queue and went off in search of tea.

The bay was dead calm. A group of cyclists passed us on their way to a day of touring the islands. Robbie—a ferry traveler for most of his life—saw the name of our boat, the Hebridean Isles, and offered his usual blunt assessment: "Aye, we've got the Hebridean. It's old, but it's a good boat. I used to take it from Kennacraig to Islay all the time when I'd go play Machrie."

The Hebridean Isles is a massive ship with a full restaurant, coffee bar, and several levels of lounge areas and decks. A few minutes after we slowly pulled away from Oban, we walked to the top deck to take in the panoramic views of the Sound of Kerrera. Robbie pointed out Scottish professional golfer Robert MacIntyre's house in the distance. Emerging from the Sound, we passed along the southern coast of Mull and into the open Atlantic. There is golf, and there is ferry golf. The sense of adventure and anticipation that comes with ferry golf is a special and unique pleasure.

It was around 11:30 am when we landed at the small ferry terminal at Scalasaig, the main (only) village on Colonsay. The tiny community consists of a small grocery shop/post office, a gin distillery, and a bookstore—perhaps I had found the ideal place. A lone sheep stood on top of a rock, staring down at us. We went into the well-stocked shop to get a drink. The clerk was slightly annoyed when I tried to pay with £10. The Colonsay Hotel sits on the hill overlooking the bay and the village. It was 65 degrees and there wasn't a cloud in the sky, so we decided to bypass the hotel and go straight to Isle of Colonsay Golf Course. It was about three miles from the ferry terminal, on the opposite side of the narrow island.

Colonsay is an island of only 15 square miles, with about 140 full-time residents. For such a small, isolated outpost of humanity, it has a somewhat violent ancient history, with Vikings seizing control of the island around 900 AD, followed by the Norse kings. Various highland clans battled for rule of the islands, with the McDonalds of Islay, known as the Lords of the Isles, seizing power from Clan MacLean in the 13th century. Clan Campbell took control over most of the western islands in the late 1600s, following a series of bloody battles in Kintyre with Clan MacDougall. The Campbells sold Colonsay to the McNeill family, who were the "Lairds" of the island until the early 20th century. The island operated as a series of "crofts," with the tenants or "crofters" paying yearly taxes to the laird for a small home to live in and the privilege of farming the land of the croft.

On Colonsay, the relationship was largely benevolent between the crofters and the mostly absentee lairds. The remnants of this old system remain even today. The family of the old lairds remains the largest landowner on the island. The island is still divided generally by its 17 crofts. Generations of Colonsay residents know the families of each croft almost as well as their own. John McPhee, in his seminal 1970 book *The Crofter and the Laird*, wrote that "Colonsay is less like a small town than like a large lifeboat."

Not far past the hotel, the road quickly became a very narrow single track. The verges were grown high and close, creating the effect of driving through a tunnel. We traveled over cattle grates, stopping often to avoid oblivious sheep in the middle of the road. Suddenly, the verges would open to stunning vistas of emerald-green fields. It was a Southern Hebridean dream world. Now there was an ancient churchyard, where unknown sailors found on the shores of Colonsay during the two world wars were laid to rest. We passed the island's only primary school: a small, tidy building. When island children reach the 9th grade, they must attend boarding school on the mainland in Oban. The way of life on Colonsay seems both so challenging and foreign, and yet seemingly idyllic and perfect. Thinking of all the years of time I had spent in the car commuting to and from my office, I was suddenly jealous of the crofters and this isolated, beautiful world.

As we approached the course, the landscape opened to a vast, rocky machair covered in grazing sheep. The machair tumbled down to a large crescent-shaped beach—the next land to the west is North America. There was space for a few cars in a small gravel car park next to the sign for Isle of Colonsay Golf Course. An honesty box attached to the sign contained a few scorecards and pencils. Robbie walked over to read a notice next to the box. He said, "The greens fee is £10 for all day, or you can join the club for £60, Jim. It says you can pay at the hotel if you want to join."

Looking out over the improbable scene of flags, sheep, rocky machair, and golden beach spread about below us, I made a split-second decision: "Fuck it, I'm joining."

Robbie let out the biggest laugh of the day. "Aye."

There was a small diagram of the course layout on the front of the scorecard, which we studied and debated for a few minutes before deciding we had deciphered the routing of the opening three holes. There was barely a 5-mph wind, and the cloudless sky held the promise of continual sunshine, which has to be a rare occurrence on this brutally exposed mass of rock, grass, and sand in the Atlantic.

Machair is a Gaelic word describing a fertile, low-lying, grassy plain. On the entire planet, it only exists on the exposed western coasts of Ireland and Scotland. It's believed that the golf course was first laid out in 1775 when Archibald MacNeill was the laird. The turf on this ancient golfing ground was perfect. Springy and resilient, it made a hollow thumping sound when struck with a club, and the ball sits up just as if it was begging to be hit. It's the type of turf that seems to give you energy as you walk on it. As we lined up our approach shots to the first green, there were four sheep lying in the sun around the tattered yellow flag.

"This place is perfect," I said quietly, almost to myself. Robbie, only a few feet away, replied, "I had a feeling you would love it here."

The 4th tee is dramatic and thrilling. It's perched high above the massive beach—Traigh An Tobair Fhuair—and the rocky cove. There was a young couple walking in the sand with a very excited black dog: the only other sign of human life we had seen since leaving the ferry terminal. We stood for a minute in silence and observed the scene. Sensing the special nature of this spot, Robbie took my photo on the tee. We continued along, playing our usual friendly match, running the ball along the ground to greens often covered in rabbit scrapes and occupied by relaxing sheep.

A local rule on the scorecard read:

> SCRAPES AND BOLT HOLES: Relief can be taken and ball dropped, without penalty, within one club's length, not nearer the hole. A drop without penalty can be taken for balls known to be lost down rabbit holes, or if taken by a raven.

We let our shots fly from the elevated tee to the machair below, avoiding the ravens and scattering sheep in the process.

The 6th hole, called Vikings Grave, has a tee situated atop a rocky escarpment. It is almost a rock-climbing exercise to reach the hitting area. Once you reach the summit, you notice that the hole is aligned with an ancient burial cairn on a clifftop in the distance. "Look at that, Jim," Robbie said in awe, "that has probably been there for 1,500 years." It's a fun, 301-yard par four, with the green situated over a rise that renders a blind approach shot. Robbie hit a beautiful, low punch shot to about 10 feet.

The 7th through 10th holes extend into a narrow and hidden area on the opposite side of the Colonsay airstrip. The 8th is a brilliant, straight-uphill, 236-yard par four to a green located in the middle of natural blow out bunkers created by sheep attempting to escape the wind. The 206-yard, par-three 9th is played back down the hill, to a green located right next to another (smaller) beach. As we putted out, three cows walked slowly along the edge of the surf. I laughed out loud at the sheer *Alice in Wonderland* nature of it all.

The 11th through the 14th are just simply great, fun golf holes. I do not care if the greens only get mowed twice a month and the maintenance is largely done by sheep. The 260-yard par-four 11th, called Sand Dunes, plays slightly downhill and along the water to a green set at the base of a massive rock formation, which (of course) you must scale to get to the 12th tee. The 324-yard par four plays out toward Dun Gallain and the ocean beyond, with yet another cairn located on the rocky hill in the distance.

Adjacent to the 12th green is a pile of rocks in the shape of a Viking longboat. Robbie speculated that this was a type of cairn used to mark the burial of a Viking chief, who were often buried in their longboats. We played back over the ancient burial marker to the green of the 161-yard, par-three 13th. This green is the high point of this part of the course. It may be the most remote and haunting spot in golf. The 14th, a short par five, plays back down the hill to a green that is completely hidden behind some interesting mounds and rocks. The entire stretch of holes is as good as anything I've played. This type of golf is clearly not for everyone, but if you love history and like an adventure, then you must figure out a way to visit the Isle of Colonsay Golf Course in your lifetime.

As we were walking down the 14th, Robbie called out to me from across the fairway.

"Jim, come look at this."

I made my way over to see him pointing down at a large rabbit hole. Inside the hole, a foot or so underground, was an old, British-size Dunlop 65 golf ball partially embedded in the sand.

"You can have it. Take it home and put it in your office. I just wanted you to see it," he said. I reached down and pulled out the old ball, which must've been at least 50 years old. It was remarkably intact.

The last few holes took us back into the more pleasantly rolling machair. We were enjoying every minute and playing reasonably well. There was still no sign of any other golfers on the course.

"Let's finish this the right way," I said, as we teed off on the 18th, a demanding par five that played to a green set perfectly among the rocks at the upper level of the car park. We had taken our time to enjoy this round, stopping often to take videos or photos or just to sit and talk for a minute. The sun was getting low in the west. We both holed out for par and ceremoniously removed our caps to shake hands.

"Well played, Robbie. That was incredible."

"Aye, I enjoyed that, Jim."

We checked into our rooms at the Colonsay Hotel, booking a table for dinner at 8:30, and took a few minutes to get settled. I met my friend in the lovely downstairs bar for a pint, which we were encouraged to take out to the perfect hotel garden to wait for our table. There was plenty of time to recount the round and, amazingly, we remembered virtually every hole in detail. I had the old Dunlop 65 in my pocket. I took it out and handed it to Robbie. We speculated on how long it might have been down that rabbit hole on the ancient machair.

The friendly hotel manager stopped by our garden table to ask how we were getting on. At this point, the pints were going down easy. I told him that I wanted to join the golf club, and he quickly returned with an application form and a member's bag tag. I immediately completed the brief application and returned it to him with three crisp £20 notes.

"I reckon I am the first member of Isle of Colonsay Golf Club from Alabama," I said somewhat proudly and perhaps a bit too loudly—eliciting genuine laughter from Robbie, the manager, and the table next to ours.

Before leaving the table, our host mentioned that there were fresh oysters on the menu, caught that very morning on the other side of the island. The meal we had in the Colonsay Hotel restaurant was excellent: simple, fresh food, expertly prepared. I will never forget how relaxed and happy Robbie was that night. It allowed me to block out my feelings of guilt and grief. I could just enjoy being with a friend. Americans often take all the things that we are able to do for granted, without even really thinking about it. Robbie had used precious vacation days from work to join me on a trip to the edge of the earth. It made me happy that he was having so much fun.

Guilt can be an overwhelming emotion after the death of a child. There is the responsibility you feel as a parent for failing to protect your child, no matter what age they might have been. A question constantly haunts your thoughts and dreams: *what could I have done differently?*. It might be the most crippling component of the grief. There's also the guilt that you feel from still being alive. It can feel wrong to take enjoyment from anything. This night, sitting in the beautiful back garden of the Colonsay Hotel, I was just a normal person again.

The ferry to Oban departed the next morning at 11:30. After our breakfast, we paid our compliments to the wonderful hotel manager and decided to explore the rest of the island for a couple of hours. Once we passed the golf course, the road once again became tunnel-like, with the verges arching over the carriageway, almost blocking out the light. We eventually came to a clearing with a small sign announcing Kiloran Beach. There was room on the verge for two or three cars.

The sun of the previous day was long gone, and the temperature had dropped precipitously to about 45 degrees Fahrenheit, which seemed sub-arctic in comparison to the day before.

There was a beautifully crafted, wooden gate leading to a path that went down to Kiloran Bay and yet another stunning, hidden beach. A few feet inside the fence sat a lovely memorial bench that had been placed to honor a longtime island native. The waves were crashing heavily in the surf below, and the wind was howling like the ghost of the Lord of The Isles was coming to collect his yearly rent. Robbie had gone ahead. Just as I walked through the gate, a young calf came strolling around the corner of thick bushes and passed in front of me. I looked to my left, in the direction from which it had come. The largest black cow I have ever seen was about 30 feet away and heading straight for me.

"Jim! Quick! get over here behind this bench! Hurry! That cow will trample you to death and then you'll be dead-like, and there will be nothing to be done for you."

When I reached the relative safety of the bench, the massive animal passed by on the other side of the structure, glancing at us menacingly.

"A cow is not your friend, Jim. They are mean, especially the big black ones. Mean, I tell you. You can never come between one of those things and its calf. That was a close call."

My friend had just saved me from certain death by marauding cows on the Isle of Colonsay. I am pretty sure he was being serious, but there's always an element of dry humor with most Scots. Always one to look for the levity in most situations, I said, "Well, thank God you saved me, Robbie. I really want a crab sandwich at the Green Seafood Shack in Oban this afternoon."

9

GAELIC FOR BEACH

"My heart's in the Highlands, my heart is not here.
My heart's in the Highlands, a-chasing a deer."
—Robert Burns, "My Heart's in the Highlands" (1789)

The lunch queue line was lengthy at "The Original Green Shack" next to the bustling Oban ferry terminal. The staff operated with a furiously restrained and efficient intensity, serving fresh local oysters, langoustines, prawns, mussels, and sandwiches with remarkable speed. There are a few seats, but most people stand and eat. Robbie insisted that I get the Famous Prawn Sandwich to takeaway for dinner back in Lochgilphead later that evening.

We spent the afternoon touring Oban. On top of Battery Hill overlooking the picturesque seaside town sits an imposing arched granite structure: McCaig's Folly. It's visible from almost everywhere and has become sort of a *de facto* symbol of the area. A local banker planned and designed the structure in 1897. He ran out of money during construction. Only the massive arched outer walls remain. Taking in the panoramic views of the town and bay below, I felt a small bit of sadness for John Stuart McCaig. He never completed his dream project.

A break was needed from the golf, but we could not resist a visit to Glencruitten. It's where emerging Scottish golf legend Robert MacIntyre learned to play the game. In the clubhouse, I noticed his name was on the wall as Junior Club Champion for four consecutive years. The friendly club secretary, Bryan Livingston, showed us a MacIntyre signed flag from the recent Open Championship. "We display a few things like this, but the last thing Bob wants is for this place to become some kind of shrine to him," said our friendly host.

Robbie had to run by his shop when we got back to Lochgilphead around 8 pm. There was an older man outside working on a large lawnmower when we arrived.

"That's John that works for me. He's a mechanic-like. Can fix anything." Robbie introduced me to his friend and co-worker.

"Aye, Robbie told me you were coming on holiday. How did you get on at Colonsay?," asked the man known locally as "The Fixer."

"It was lovely. Everything about it"

"Aye, it would be."

The two old friends caught up on the last few days of work. It was just a discussion about various historic sites they looked after, but I could have listened to them talk all night.

It was almost time for me to leave Kintyre and allow my friend to get back to his normal work routine. We ate our famous prawn sandwiches from Oban in his den. Davy Wilson, Robbie's father, came by for a visit. Mr. Wilson was 81 years old but looked like he could walk 36 holes at a moment's notice. A former electrician, he still plays occasionally at Lochgilphead Golf Club. He asked where I would be traveling over the next two weeks. Many of the places that I mentioned were in the far north of Scotland: areas of the country that he had never even visited. He was a kind, well-spoken man and reminded me of my own father. It was obvious that Robbie was proud of him. Their love for each other was also evident.

"I hope Robbie has looked after you, Jim. I'm so sorry for the loss of your boy."

"Thank you. Yes, sir, he has. He's been great to me. I'll be back in two weeks if he's up for more."

"Robbie, he called me sir! Finally getting the respect I deserve around here."

The next morning, I decided on the spur of the moment to visit the Isle of Bute. Robbie knew all the ferries and gave me instructions for each one. They were all drive-up sailings: Tarbert to Portavadie and Colintraive to Rhubodach. Before I left, we discussed meeting up on Oban in a few days to play Traigh on my way north. Robbie wanted to visit his daughter's new house in Fort William. She had graciously offered to let me stay the night, if needed, on my travels.

The ferry crossing at Tarbert was the roughest of the trip. Water crashed over both sides of the relatively small boat all the way across Loch Fyne. I called the Victoria Hotel in Rothesay and booked a room. The drive from Portavadie along the Kyles of Bute was breathtaking. Thickly wooded hillsides sloped sharply down to the narrow sea channel, hundreds of feet below. The surface of the water was smooth, the only disruption coming from the wake of a bright red sailboat heading north. Seeing a small sign for Kyles of Bute Golf Club, I turned down a single-track dirt road. After many wrong turns, I finally found the course with the help of a friendly sheep farmer. I walked out to see a few holes. A green on a hilltop stood in front of a fairway cascading down to the sea. The view from my vantage point toward the Kyles was worth the short detour. Scotland had the greatest collection of nine-hole courses in the world. No other country even comes close.

From the ferry landing at Rhubodach, it was a short drive along sheep-filled roads to Rothesay. The main town on the Isle of Bute, it had become a popular holiday destination in the Victorian area. The elaborate architecture of the seaside town certainly looked the part. I parked by the ferry terminal to have a look around. Two west highland terriers were perched in the open window of a bright blue van, patiently waiting for their owner to return from a shop. A market displayed fresh leeks, corn, and tomatoes on the sidewalk. The storefront for an old-fashioned sweets shop offered Buckfast Creams, Flying Saucers, and Lucky Tatties. There was a large community putting green across the street from my hotel. My room would not be ready until 4 pm, so I decided to visit Rothesay Golf Club. Robbie had spoken highly of it, having played there in his junior golf days.

Located on the hills above town, the imposing and elegant Rothesay clubhouse had just the right amount of old world, slightly run-down elegance. It's situated by the 18th green and 1st tee: holes which run parallel to each other up and down one of the steepest inclines I've ever seen on a golf course. My 54-year-old legs, having walked over 100 miles in the last week, suddenly felt very heavy. I noticed four golf carts (referred to as buggies in Scotland) parked by the clubhouse. This would have been unthinkable 10 years earlier.

Preparations were ongoing for a big Seniors Open, in the Starters office located in the clubhouse basement. I had not made prior arrangements to play. Hoping the nice lady behind the counter would take pity on an American visitor, I asked if it might be possible to play—and perhaps hire one of the buggies.

"Oh, aye, you can play, right enough. The tee is open just now. I'm afraid all the buggies are booked for this afternoon."

My heart sank at the thought of climbing that sheer cliff on the opening hole.

"No, wait. Someone has canceled. I can let you have one."

I was about to ride in a golf cart in Scotland for the first time in my life. I felt guilty, but also relieved that I would be able to play a course I really wanted to see. I paid my greens fee before she could change her mind.

Located in the hills high above town, Rothesay Golf Club is visually stunning. Once the heights of the first green are reached, the panoramic vistas never stop. It's also fun: measuring 5,400 yards long, but it's a challenging par of 68. There are wonderful blind shots on the 3rd, 12th, and 15th holes. Golf partially lost its way when it somehow became an unwritten requirement that courses must be a par 72 and 7,000 yards long—and blind shots somehow became "unfair." I blame this on the influence of professional golf. Would that we were all lucky enough to have a course like Rothesay to play every day.

The 1st and 18th are a perfect microcosm of the wild fantasy that is often Scottish golf. The 1st is a straight uphill par four of 280 yards, and the 18th is a straight downhill par three of 240 yards. They are mirror images of each other. Par is largely irrelevant in Scotland and often seemingly arbitrary—what matters is beating your opponent. It's a great "1st and 18th" combination, in the grand tradition of the Old Course, Fraserburgh, North Berwick, Machrihanish, Dunaverty, and many others.

I felt an impending sense of shame at taking the golf cart, but there were not many players out on the course. That was a relief. My lifelong Scottish golf credentials could have been summarily revoked. I caught up to a twosome walking along the path to the 8th hole, a stunning 183-yard, downhill par three. I immediately began my apology.

"Hello, sorry to run up on you guys. I've got an unfair advantage with this buggy." I was surprised to hear an American accent respond. That wasn't something I had been expecting.

"No problem at all. This is great, is it not?," a fully American accent replied. He gestured around in a 360-degree direction as he spoke, "there is nothing like this in the States."

"You are right about that," I replied.

Once through the two-ball from Illinois, I had the rest of the course to myself. I took my time to try to understand the strategy of each hole—which were both fun and challenging, while not overly penal. At the downhill 168-yard par three 13th, curiously called The Tank, I came upon the greenskeeper. He was hard at work on the bunkers surrounding the steeply sloping green. A few odd looking low rectangular structures sat just left of where he worked.

"Hello, how are you getting on? Enjoying the course?"

I had the usual suspicion that word had gotten out from the clubhouse that a random American was out playing, in a cart no less. I also may have let it slip to the Starter that I do a wee bit of golf writing. Whatever the circumstances, I never miss a chance to have a conversation with the man in charge of the course.

"It's beautiful. I'm really enjoying it."

"Aye, it's a nice course. People here get spoiled because they play it so much. You hear all the time that it's not a championship course, but let's see them shoot par out here today in this wind. I'm trying to get everything ready for the Seniors Open tomorrow."

The remaining holes were played over wildly undulating, hilltop land. I felt energized as I played back down the mountain to the 18th green, maybe in part due to the cart saving my legs. The hole played straight downwind. From 240 yards, a 7 iron from the elevated tee was easily enough club to reach the green. I could easily imagine a ball striking the clubhouse with such a strong tailwind. There were two shadowy figures watching me finish from the clubhouse windows. I was relieved to get down in two for par.

My gallery, two older members, were seated by the windows sipping a pint. In search of a late lunch, I removed my hat and nodded in their direction. One of them spoke to me.

"Well done down the last."

"I got lucky."

At the bar, I asked the steward if I could get some lunch.

"I've only got soup just now. Will that do?"

After three hours out on the course on a cool, windy, 50-degree day, that sounded perfect. A few minutes later I had my tomato-basil soup. Looking out the window, I saw the two Americans playing down the 18th. They shook hands after holing out. I wondered what had brought them to play golf on the Isle of Bute, with all the travel challenges of the global pandemic.

Back in town, I checked into the Victorian Hotel. The restaurant was closed due to Covid. I decided to have another walk around town. The storefronts were all painted in bright red, green, and blue. I stuck my head in a pub called The Criterion. Two men were sitting at the dimly lit bar, with a dog sleeping at their feet. They nodded in my direction. A few streets over, a sign for the Golfer's Bar looked intriguing. There were not many people in the dark, wood-paneled pub. I ordered a pint of Tennent's and struck up a conversation with the bartender, a friendly man named Jimmy. He explained the origins of the name—the pub had once served as the clubhouse for the original Rothesay Golf Club. It was a long-lost James Braid design that was now the site of council estates.

I took my pint and sat at a table by the front door, with a view of the busy sidewalk. It was a pleasant sunny evening, and people started to come in with their dogs. It was nice not to think and simply watch the endless parade of happy canines. Two old ladies sitting next to me were drinking half-pints of cider. At some point in the evening, the pub was full, and Jimmy broke into a surprisingly good acapella version of *Purple Rain*. The happy crowd joined in loudly during the chorus.

The next morning, I had a full Scottish breakfast in the Victorian—at the bay window overlooking the community putting green on Rothesay harbor. On the walk back the night before, sev-eral families had been on the green. There were grandparents playing with small grandchildren, who ran after their balls as they rolled toward the hole. Golf is simply part of the fabric of life in this country.

There are two routes from Rothesay to Bute Golf Club. I decided to take the more direct line on the way there. The B881 winds through lovely farmland, with more sheep than cars on the carriageway. After a few miles, I saw a small sign by an open gate with a cattle grate:

Welcome to
BUTE GOLF CLUB
Founded 1888
A UNIQUE NINE-HOLE COURSE

The greens fee was £15, whether for nine holes, 18, or all day. I liked this place immediately.

The single-track dirt path continued about half a mile, through farmland with old stone crofts, before ending in a small empty car park. A narrow path wound through gorse to an elaborate green Victorian shed, which serves as the clubhouse. As I approached the small structure, a disembodied stentorian voice suddenly boomed out—like the man behind the curtain in the Wizard of Oz.

"Welcome to Bute Golf Club. Please enter your tracking details and submit payment through the mail slot. Enjoy your round."

After overcoming the initial shock, I realized it was a motion activated system. I slipped £20 through the slot, looking through the small window into a beautiful wood paneled locker room. It looked unchanged since the Victorian tourists started visiting the island over 130 years ago.

It was a cool, windy morning, with interludes of blinding sun. Across the Firth of Clyde, the peak of Goatfell on Arran was bathed in a golden, misty light. Standing on the 1st tee, I felt pleasantly isolated from the rest of the world.

The opening trio of holes at Bute are the best on the course. The 1st, a 336-yard par four, starts us out to the Firth, with gorse in play on both sides. It's a testing drive to start the day. The 2nd, called Stravannan, is a 324-yard par four. The fairway is bisected diagonally by an ancient rock wall, about 250 yards from the tee. You must decide to lay up with an iron or attempt to carry the wall with a driver. The large, undulating green is hard by the rocky coast of the Firth. The sun broke through once more as I approached the old wall. The green suddenly became a bright shade of emerald set against a vast cyan backdrop.

The last member of this unique triumvirate, the 3rd is a unique 162-yard par three along the rocky coastline. A small burn snakes in front of the green on its way to the Firth, forbidding a run-up shot from the tee. The remaining holes move away from the shore and into nicely rolling farmland. There are several blind shots and an abundance of gorse to keep things interesting.

Coming down the 9th, I saw an old man with a small boy and girl walking down the 1st fairway. It looked like a grandfather out for a morning game with his wee grandchildren. Like the putting green in Rothesay the night before, the kids were running between shots. Those happy children, with their grandfather strolling patiently behind, made me smile. I sat down to rest briefly on a bench by the clubhouse/shed, once again setting off the somewhat disturbing voice of the wizard behind the curtain. I looked out over the links of Bute, wanting to remember this morning. The only sound was the wind blowing through the gorse and waves crashing on the rocks.

I thought again of Jordan in those early years when the two of us played so much golf together. The pure joy of hitting a golf ball was all that mattered to him back then—and even that might have been secondary to the post-round hot dog in the clubhouse. He would talk all week about where we might go play on Saturday. I always let him choose the course. Almost every night, when I got home from work, he would be in the front yard chipping plastic golf balls. I now realized that he wanted me to see him practicing. He wanted to be there waiting for me, after my torturous 90-minute commute. The thought was heartbreaking. Tears started to roll down my face as the happy threesome faded into the distance.

I decided to take the coastal route back to Rothesay. It was still early in the morning. At Kingarth, not far from the course, Google Maps sent me onto a narrow single-track road. It continued through dense woodland and periods of open farmland for about five miles, where I saw a sign for Mount Stuart. It appeared to be a historical site. With nowhere to be for the rest of the day, I turned into the car park. There were a few people walking down a winding forest path, so I followed along.

Eventually the trail emerged at a massive granite Victorian Gothic structure. It was surrounded by 3,000 acres of immaculately kept grounds that tumbled gently down to the sea. My architectural curiosity took over and I paid the £15 entry fee. Mount Stuart, as I learned, was the family seat of the Stewarts of Bute, direct descendants of King Robert II of Scotland and Robert the Bruce. There was a guided tour starting, but I wanted to walk around by myself. The lovely marble and tile chapel was being set up for a wedding. A father somewhere in Scotland had probably spent a year's wages on the ceremony. He should be happy he had the chance to do it.

The reddish-brown stonework is a marvel of masonry construction, with cast iron brackets, trim, and details of every conceivable design.

With all our modern advancements in construction and design due to 3D modeling, nothing built today even remotely compares to the stunning craftsmanship of Mount Stuart. The interior, if possible, is even more impressive. A great marble hall is capped by a ceiling displaying celestial bodies of the nighttime sky. Granite, stained glass, wood millwork, and inlaid tile rival the palace of Versailles. I felt a sense of mystery and intrigue, as if the Knights Templar might have hidden the Holy Grail somewhere in the library.

I left Rothesay the next day to travel northwest. I had nothing planned, other than a room booked in Oban for the night. My driver shaft had inexplicably broken on the last hole at Bute. Robbie mentioned that there was a great pro shop at Helensburgh Golf Club, about 30 minutes northwest of the Glasgow airport. I called from the road and the friendly pro, Fraser Hall, said he could "sort it, no bother." While Fraser changed out the shaft, I stocked up on balls and gloves. I sat outside on the patio for a few minutes, seriously considering giving the lovely looking James Braid layout a go. My body needed a rest, so common sense prevailed for once.

On the way out of Helensburgh, I saw a sign for Hill House—the masterpiece of the great Scottish architect Charles Rennie MacKintosh. With most of the day still ahead of me, I decided to make a visit. While studying architecture at Mississippi State, Mackintosh had been my favorite architect. I wrote a thesis paper on Hill House and the Glasgow School of Art, his two most well-known designs. I had passed the Helensburgh turn off at least 30 times over the years but had never taken time to visit Hill House.

The drive through a residential neighborhood was unremarkable—until I saw a giant steel superstructure where Hill House was meant to be located. I assumed it was closed for repairs and started to turn around to leave. A few people were walking into the giant steel cage, so I parked on the street. It quickly became apparent that the steel superstructure had been constructed as a weather barrier to protect the fragile stucco exterior of the 120-year-old home. It was masterfully done, with catwalks extending well above the roof. These walkways afforded views of the intricate roof that would have otherwise been impossible.

A fellow architect who worked at the site was kind enough to give me a brief history. She explained why the structure had to be built and mentioned it had won a national design award. Once inside, everything was perfectly preserved, just as it would have been in 1908. Hill House is a tour-de-force of design. The level to which Mackintosh integrated the design of every detail of the residence—furniture, door hardware, light fixtures, plumbing—exceeds even that of architectural masters like Frank Lloyd Wright and Carlo Scarpa. I spent almost two hours walking around the house. Maybe it was an effort to make up for all the years of bypassing Hill House to get somewhere quickly for golf.

I started north on the A82 to Oban. Instead of taking the most direct route through Crianlarich, I took the A83 turn off toward Inverary. Loch Fyne Oysters lay along that path, and it had been several hours since breakfast at the Victoria. In 45 minutes, I was sitting outside at a table on Loch Fyne eating raw oysters and steamed langoustines. The bar had red and green Tabasco sauce. It was one of the best days I had ever spent in Scotland, without a single golf shot having been struck.

At 7:30 am the next day, Robbie was waiting at the petrol station across the street from my Oban bed and breakfast. I admired the fact that he was never late for anything. I followed him up the A828 to Fort William, where we planned to meet Shannon's boyfriend, Gregor, and his mate named Ryan. Gregor was on leave from the UK Army and played golf every chance he could. They were waiting for us at the public car park on Loch Linnhe, just as you get into town. We could not fit all the golf bags into one car, so Robbie volunteered to drive us.

"We'll take my wee car, Jim. You may struggle to keep up with Gregor. He drives like a bat out of hell."

The hour-long drive from Fort William to Traigh was a surprisingly easy one, with nice wide roads that Robbie credited to money from the European Union. "No more of that now, I'm afraid," he said, shaking his head. The car park was across the road, by Traigh

Beach. Before we could reach the small, perfect white clubhouse, Robbie was greeted by an older gentleman on the 1st tee. They had met briefly on a previous visit, playing a few holes together. He accosted Robbie like an old friend. We talked for a few minutes about the condition of the course. He was interested in where I had played on my trip. After a pleasant conversation, he said, "right, come with me," and strode quickly into the clubhouse where the club secretary was seated behind a large desk.

"Elizabeth, I'm signing on these two boys as my guests today. Please take care of them." Then he shook our hands with a "Well, that's me. Enjoy your round," and he was gone.

I had expected an honesty box. The secretary was performing her duties with an admirable seriousness. "Gentlemen, that will be £20 for a day ticket," she said officiously. Robbie and I each handed her a £20 note. "No, no it's £20 for the both of you," she replied. It was only £10 each for a day of golf at Traigh. The kindness of strangers in Scotland never fails.

Golf has been played at Traigh since 1900, but for a large part of its existence it was a private course for a local farmer and his friends. In 1993, the landowner, Jack Stewart, invited a well-known member of the R&A, John Salvesen, to rework the nine-hole course. Salvesen had previously consulted on many course improvements throughout the UK. If Traigh is any indication, he is a talented course designer.

The 1st hole at Traigh plays straight uphill to a plateau green. There's no room for error. Short, left and long are nothing but high bent grasses. It's only 130 yards, but it's as intimidating a start to a round of golf as can be found. It would be just as easy to make a seven as a two. From the heights of the 1st green, it was easy to see why Robbie insisted that I visit Traigh. The beach, the Atlantic Ocean and the rocky Isle of Eigg was an incredible panorama below us.

Traigh never lets down after the tricky opener. The 2nd is the strongest hole on the course. From a pulpit tee, the drive is played blind over a massive dune to a fairway that we can only hope is out there. There's also an option to play way left to an alternate fairway, well below the level of the tee. On the direct line, any tee shot that falls short of carrying the dune is likely a goner. The 2nd shot could be anything from a 7 iron to a 3 wood on this 452-yard par five. From the hidden plateau of the upper fairway, the shot into the green is also blind. The green is a wonderful punchbowl set in the dunes. It gathers shots from all sides. I don't think I have ever seen another hole quite like it. It's unforgettable.

The remaining holes are simply pure fun. The Bridge, the 5th hole, is lovely 135-yard downhill par three. A pitching wedge or 4 iron is played over a wide burn to a green with only the mighty Atlantic as a backdrop. Playing back uphill on the 6th, a sideways blowing rainstorm suddenly came out of nowhere. The sunshine of the first five holes was gone. We quickly ducked into a nearby shelter. A man seated inside on the long wooden bench invited us in. I sat next to him and he introduced himself as John Gibbs.

After the obvious topic of the weather was discussed, John began to talk about Traigh: "Traigh is Gaelic for beach. I've always found that a bit ironic, since we only have two bunkers on the course. In fairness, the course is mostly located on old sand dunes. We don't have a full time greenskeeper just now, so the greens aren't as good as they should be. Even so, I'd rather be here than just about anywhere. I play several times a week."

I told him I hoped to write about the course at some point. "You're a writer? Well, I write a wee bit as well," he said. "I'm a salmon fisherman and I've written about fly fishing for a few publications in Scotland. I find that there's a correlation between golf and fishing. They are both about your relationship with nature. What could be better than walking around Traigh or spending a morning in a lovely river? Catching a fish is secondary, much like the score in golf is almost irrelevant."

A hoolie (Scottish slang for a strong wind and rainstorm) that had blown in vanished almost as quickly as it had arrived. The sun had already started to return. I shook John Gibbs' hand and promised to find some of his writing. He went ahead to the nearby 7th tee and was out of sight by the time we finished the 6th hole. We continued our friendly match. Gregor could hit it miles but was sometimes wildly offline. Robbie was playing his normal steady game. Ryan, a talented joiner from Spean Bridge, was happy to hit the occasional good shot. I hung back to watch the group on the 9th, a par three that plays back down the hill we climbed at the start. The three of them walked closely together, silhouetted in the sun, with the small green islands of Eigg and Rum in the ocean beyond. It was the ideal image of a friendly Sunday game on the coast of Scotland.

Gregor was familiar with the area and suggested we visit nearby Camusdarach Beach. After a near-mile walk through a narrow sandy path, we emerged on a hidden golden strand. There were two families playing a game of football and dogs chasing balls in the surf. We went on to Mallaig for a late lunch of prawns and a pint for Ryan and I, the two non-drivers. Robbie insisted I try something called a "99": a soft serve ice cream in a waffle cone with a long stick of dark chocolate protruding at a 45-degree angle.

We drove back to Fort William, saying goodbye to Ryan in the car park. After tea at Shannon and Gregor's house, Robbie had to get home to Lochgilphead. I was to stay the night with Shannon and Gregor in their lovely new home. Since it never seems to get dark in Scotland, the three of us decided to get in another round at a local nine-holer in South Ballachulish.

The course, formerly called Dragon's Tooth (now called the unfortunate American-sounding name Woodlands), is in the shadow of Sgorr Dhearg, a 3,360-foot peak of the Beinn a' Bheitir, one of the most dramatic mountains in Scotland. Shannon, a former player on the Scottish national Shinty team, was tall, outgoing, and a strong ball striker. "Shinty is a rough game, but I'm quite a large girl so it's never been a problem for me," she said, without a hint of self-consciousness. Gregor was somewhat more reticent, but his love of golf was obvious. He had recently run to the top of Ben Nevis, the highest peak in Scotland. This wasn't a man to be taken lightly. They had opened their new home to me, so I paid for their golf. It was the least I could do.

These two had never met me before this day, but they took me in like we were old friends. I loved playing with them—it was nice to see two people with their entire lives ahead. But it came with melancholy. Jordan would never be able to play golf with his girlfriend on the spur of the moment on a summer Sunday night; but the moment passed without me breaking down completely. Gregor blasted his drive an unimaginable distance off the first tee. Shannon, not to be outdone, hit one long and straight, just past her boyfriend's ball. They were playing out of the same golf bag.

At the wild, 90-degree dogleg of the 3rd hole, the fairway dropped down to a lower level. We all hit good drives. When we got to the corner, I noticed a massive red deer grazing by the green, about 100 yards away. It seemed unconcerned by anything we were doing and when we all hit our shots to the green it nonchalantly strolled into the woods, where a lovely river ran into Loch Linnhe. I putted out first and went ahead of Shannon and Gregor, who were hitting a few practice putts. As I went over the bridge, I looked down. The deer was staring straight up at me. I froze. The deer did not move at all, he just kept looking at me. I choose to believe that the universe is not totally explainable. I stood on the edge of that stone bridge and looked at this beautiful creature for at least a minute. I choose to believe it was a sign from my son.

There was a calmness and sense of recognition in those huge, and seemingly ancient, brown eyes. I could not look away. The bridge was close to the A828, but no cars came by. It was dead silent in the gathering twilight, except for the sound of the clear water flowing over the rocks below. An eternity, and only a second, passed on the gently curving span. For the first time since Jordan's death, I felt— for just those few moments—that maybe there was a reason for me to keep going. There were no answers yet, but maybe I needed to stay open to looking for them.

When Shannon and Gregor walked up, the deer did not run. He just slowly faded into the evening mist.

10

A NINE-HOLE
BILLY-GOAT LAYOUT

Banquo: *It will be rain to-night.*
First Murderer: *Let it come down.*
—William Shakespeare, *Macbeth*

I slipped out of the house quietly, before my two young friends were awake. They had shown me so much kindness, the least I could do is not disturb them at 6 am on a Monday. Shannon's shinty stick was standing proudly in the corner by the front door. Traffic was almost non-existent at that time of day in Fort William. A series of roundabouts slung me north through town to the A87. At the turnoff to Lochcarron, my intended destination, there was a sign: "Isle of Skye—34 miles." I made the sudden decision to keep going.

My only concrete plan for the day was a room I had booked at the Gairloch Hotel. The nine-hole Isle of Skye Golf Club had first come to my attention in the wonderful 1993 book *Hell's Golfer* by

Scottish author Tom Morton. The few photos I had seen over the years looked intriguing.

About 45 minutes later, I was on the Skye Bridge at Kyles of Lochalsh. Opened in 1995 amid much controversy, it allowed for continuous access to the famous island. It was originally a toll bridge. This did not sit well with many island residents. There were also those that felt it would be detrimental to Skye's identity as an island. Kyles of Lochalsh had been the ferry link to Skye since the 1600s. Inevitably some of that romance and history has been lost, but the island is now one of the most popular holiday destinations in the UK. Thankfully, the tariff was lifted in 2004. It's a lovely, elegant feat of engineering. The bridge, once a source of conflict, now contributes to the experience of visiting Skye.

The car park next to the small clubhouse was empty—not surprising at 8:30 am on a normal workday. After depositing £20 in the honesty box, I was on my way. The view on the 307-yard, downhill 1st, on a clear morning, was a portent of the beauty to come. The tee was situated high in a field of colorful native plants. An ancient looking rock wall bordered the left side of the generous fairway, which tumbled downhill to a large inviting green. A CalMac ferry moved slowly across the eerily still Caol Mor on the way to the Isle of Raasay.

A theatrical, almost fantasy-like, mountainous landscape framed most of the holes at Isle of Skye. There's a large rock quarry in the distance behind the 2nd green, which admittedly detracts slightly from the proceedings. It's a necessity to maintain the roads on the island—and in the larger scheme of things, only a minor annoyance. The fantastic variety of native plants provide wonderful accents of violet, deep purple, yellow, and red. The greenskeeper, a man named John Cunningham, clearly has a deep love for the natural environment.

At the 4th tee, I noticed a smartly dressed gentleman strolling through the high fescue. He was wielding a single club like a scythe, in an apparent search for golf balls. When he saw me, he started my way. I waited on him to approach, and he spoke first: "Hello! How are you doing on this fine day?"

John Marshall, a retired teacher at Portree High School, has been a member of Isle of Skye since 1976. Most days, he is at the golf course. He is the unofficial club historian and one-man welcoming committee. I liked him immediately and was curious about why he was out walking through the rough. "I enjoy a wee chat and it makes our visitors feel welcome. And it breaks the monotony of my practice," he replied. When I mentioned that I was interested in the history of the course, he went straight into high school history teacher mode.

Over the years there had been plans to expand the course to 18 holes. The land to the north is rocky and dramatic. It already looks like a golf course. All that is needed are a few greens and tees. "We learned that what you see up there's very historic crofting land and that stopped the expansion plans," he said. There's a persistent myth that Old Tom Morris helped lay out the course on his way to Askernish with Horace Hutchinson in 1891. It's well documented that the pair stayed at Sconser Lodge—located adjacent to the course—for several days. Marshall, however, puts no credence in those rumors. "It's just a nice story."

Before I knew it, 20 minutes had passed. "I better get going," I said, shaking John Marshall's hand. "It was lovely to meet you. You should play the 5th from the back 9 tee. It's a much better hole from up there," he said in parting. At the next hole, I took his advice and climbed to the 14th tee. From there, the hole was only 129 yards, as opposed to 201 from the lower tee. It is a completely different hole. Not only is the tee shot much more manageable, you are also rewarded with a stunning view of the channel and Raasay beyond. I was suddenly striking the ball well and the round passed quickly.

The 8th hole, called Suidhisnis, was the standout of the day for me. The drive is blind and must be laid up short of a meandering burn surrounded by beautiful native plants. If the tee shot is not played far enough left, the approach shot is also blind. It's a wonderfully strategic jewel of a hole. A walk around Isle of Skye Golf Club, even with a pleasant history lesson from a former teacher, was well under two hours.

On John Marshall's advice, I had an early lunch at Deli Gasta in Broadford. Looking at the menu, I thought about how many times Jordan and I stopped for a meal following one of his tournament rounds. Many of those times, we had a victory celebration: just the two of us. In some ways, that time alone with him was more fun than the golf. If he had won or played well, the conversation flowed easily. If things had gone wrong, he would be reluctant to talk. Usually, after a few minutes had passed, we might be able to talk about what he could have done differently. It was a post-round ritual that I cherished.

One of the last tournaments he won was just a few weeks before starting his senior year of high school. It was at Highland Park in Birmingham, Alabama, a wonderful old neighborhood course with views of the downtown skyline. He shot a 68, making a birdie on the 18th hole to get in a playoff. On the first extra hole, a drivable par four, he hooked his tee shot in the rough left of the green. His competitor had driven it on the putting surface and had about 30 feet left for eagle. The situation looked bleak. After calmly studying the lie for a few seconds, he took a wedge and popped the ball straight up in the air. It bounced once and went into the cup.

There was a hamburger restaurant that Jordan loved, called Jack Brown's, just a mile from the golf course. It was usually packed, especially on a Saturday afternoon, but we found a table by the window. We talked about his victory, but even more about the prospects for the upcoming football season for the Alabama Crimson Tide. He was as happy as I had ever seen him. A few weeks later, he would be prescribed Adderall for the first time.

The friendly Scots server, probably the same age as Jordan had been that day at Highland Park, placed a Diet Coke on the table. The feelings of guilt started to creep into my mind. *How could I have let this happen to my precious son?* I should have done something. Good grades in school aren't worth the risk of taking a mind-altering, addictive drug. My wife and I both blindly trusted the psychiatrist that Jordan had been seeing. In those first few months, his grades improved drastically. It was a false sense of security. My lunch arrived, breaking my sad, solitary reverie.

A Hebridean smoked salmon sandwich restored my energy and a bit of my depressed mood. Google maps, my constant companion, showed that Lochcarron Golf Club was only 45 minutes away. A few minutes after lunch, I was back over the Skye Bridge and through Kyles of Lochalsh, I took the A890 north at Auchentyre. The road quickly became disturbingly narrow. My hard-earned Scottish driving skills of 30 years would be sorely tested over the next few days.

Jake had texted me some photos of a nine-hole course called Lochcarron a few days earlier, saying, "you should go here, Dad. It looks really hidden." *Hidden* was a code word we had always used—Jordan and Jonathan too—for something that looks interesting and unusual. There is a language that develops over time between fathers and sons. It could be through books, music, movies, or sports—or in our case, all four. I had always been close to my three boys, in a different way than my dad and I had been. We all loved the same things: the movies of the Coen Brothers and Quentin Tarantino, the music of The Velvet Underground, Led Zeppelin, and Pink Floyd, golf, and Alabama football. The thought of attending another Alabama football game with Jordan gone was now inconceivable to me. Many of the things I had always loved had become painful—a reminder of the magnitude of our loss.

I knew virtually nothing about the course at Lochcarron. One of the photos showed an old white church and cemetery in the middle of a golf course. That was all the encouragement that I needed to make a stop there on the way north to Durness. The narrow road into the village bisected the course, with three holes on the narrow strip of land by the loch and the other six located on the church side.

A small café by the loch served as the clubhouse. There was a large, noisy lunchtime crowd in the cozy dining room. At the counter, a lady who appeared to be in charge spoke to me as I entered.

"Hiya. Are you wanting some lunch?"

"No, just the golf for me."

"Aye, that will be £10 for the day. I'll show you the way to the 1st tee."

Leaving the happy diners, she led me through a group of trees to a small tee out by the road I had just come in on. From the tee on the 215-yard opener, I had no idea what was intended. The top of a flag was partially visible in the distance, but not much else. Eighty yards of semi-fairway in front of the tee ended in a tangle of burns, gorse, and the rocky beach of Loch Carron. It looked impossible.

"Where are you supposed to hit the ball?"

"The wee green is about your only option. It's quite a tricky hole to start."

The chef/starter gave me a general description of how to get around, and apologized as she left, "Sorry that we don't have a map just now." I took an 8 iron and punched it about 70 yards to the edge of the burn. From there it was a 9 iron to the hidden green by the loch. It's a beautiful, bizarre, and difficult opening hole. If Jake had been with me, he would have laughed out loud at the absurdity of it.

Lochcarron is the type of simple, fun, and inexpensive country golf that has slowly disappeared across the United States. In north Alabama alone, there are at least 10 rural courses that have closed in the last 15 years. These were places where dads took their children to learn the game—or a group of high school friends went to play a quick, cheap nine after school. Old men sat in small shack-like clubhouses and solved all the world's problems. Thankfully places like this still exist throughout Scotland.

The north side of the course wound through lovely heathland, with a clear rushing burn and plenty of gorse. The 7th, 8th, and 9th holes played around the picturesque old churchyard. It started to rain. At the 9th green, hard by the cemetery gate, a man in his mid- to late-eighties was hitting chip shots to the small round green. He wore an old-style flat cap and was the first person I had seen on the course.

"How are you today, good sir?," he asked, as I placed my bag by the green. "I was okay until this rain started," I replied.

"Aye, I'm used to it at this point in my life." His smile was infectious.

I walked across the road, stopping in the café to say goodbye to the friendly steward. I wanted her to know how much I had enjoyed being at Lochcarron.

Much of the way north to Gairloch was along Loch Maree. I drove slowly on the narrow road, stopping on the verge a few times to take in the scenery. Worn out from the day of golf and driving, I had a quick dinner in the hotel and went straight to bed. I sent Jake, Jonathan, and my wife Jaymaine several photos of Lochcarron before falling asleep. After weeks of sleeping no more than an hour at a time, playing so much golf had at least brought me to the point of exhaustion every night.

Gairloch is a small lochside village between the base of Auchtercairn and Gairloch Beach. In addition to the golf course and hotel, there are several lovely old churches and a wonderful museum. The main part of the village sits along a narrow inlet of the loch. Boats of all sizes were tethered to the side of the seawall. The old burial ground next to the course is a peaceful and lovingly kept memorial garden, where many local war veterans are buried. A sign in front of the clubhouse described Gairloch as "Possibly the best wee nine-hole course in the Highlands." I admired the use of the slight disclaimer. When I arrived at 7:30, the café/clubhouse was locked. I slipped my greens fee into the bright blue honesty box. A narrow footpath led toward an old church and the 1st tee.

I only knew slightly more about Gairloch than Lochcarron. It had received the highest recommendation from Josh Ralston at North Berwick, so I had a feeling something special might be imminent. My previous knowledge had come from a cryptic reference by the great Herbert Warren Wind in his seminal 1964 *New Yorker* story, "North to The Links of Dornoch." It was the first story I ever read on Scottish golf and solidified my developing love for the country and its links.

On a golf trip with the Scottish journalist S.L. McKinlay, the pair played Nairn, Golspie, and most famously, Dornoch. (Curiously, there was no mention of Brora in the story.) In 1964, an American traveling that far north to play golf in Scotland was something akin to driving to the moon. Toward the end of the wonderful piece, as Wind is reflecting on the trip, he mentions Gairloch:

One day, I suppose, some high voltage syndicate will build a Scottish version of our Pebble Beach along the craggy headlands of the west coast, but up to now the obvious expense of such an undertaking has frightened the developers away. Currently, the only course up north along the west coast is at Gairloch, and that one is a nine-hole billy-goat layout where most of the holes intersect each other and a single cry of "Fore!" can send all the golfers on the course diving flat on the ground. McKinlay rates it a half a thistle.

It's rare that I would question two figures so eminent as Herbert Wind and Sam McKinlay, but in the case of Gairloch they are decidedly wrong. Although Wind does sort of predict the creation of places like Castle Stuart and Kingsbarns, 40 years ahead of time.

Gairloch was a surprising revelation. To start with, the course was in immaculate condition. The fairways were flawless and fast. The greens were smooth and true. Conditioning is generally not a major deciding factor on how I rate a course, but this was almost a work of art. I met the greenskeeper near the 3rd green and told him as much.

"That's kind of you to say. The weather has been in my favor."

"Do you take care of this place by yourself?"

"Aye."

The amount of pride he had in his work was obvious. It was oddly moving to see such a small, remote course maintained as if final Open qualifying were to be held that day. I left him to his solitary task and walked on. A beautifully crafted memorial bench was located by the 4th tee. The joinery of the woodwork was stunning. It had obviously been custom built by a serious craftsman. It seemed disrespectful not to sit down for a few minutes.

It was a quiet morning. I could hear the greenskeeper's equipment humming in the distance. Not long after sitting on the bench, I received a text message from my wife. It was a drawing of Jordan's granite headstone. Under his name were two crossed golf clubs, like the symbol of the links at St. Andrews. Below the clubs were the following words: *Loving Son, Brother, Grandson, and Uncle.*

"Does this look ok to you? Your dad wants to order it today."

I stared at the image on my phone, tears forming in my eyes. "Yes," I replied.

It is wholly unnatural for a parent to approve the design of a gravestone for their child. Even after two and a half months, it was still surreal to think that Jordan was gone. The text took my mind back to the day of the funeral: something I had tried hard to block out.

We had chosen to only have a graveside service. I have always believed that some of the traditions associated with death are just too hard on those who are grieving. The sunny, windy day was not unlike so many of the days I spent watching the Hartselle High School boys golf team. I saw most of my co-workers, some of whom were like family, and many of Jordan's former teammates. Just as the minister started the eulogy, a train came roaring by. It was hard for me to remember much more than that, until a few minutes after the service ended.

When Jordan was 17, he needed a new car. Things had been going so well with school and golf, I was in the mood to give him what he wanted. He found a used BMW 325i and begged us to get it for him. It was way beyond our price range, but we bought it anyway. He loved that car. When he died, we still owed several thousand dollars on the loan—vastly more than its actual worth. Standing a few feet away from my son's grave, I felt a hand on my shoulder. I turned around to see my dad's oldest friend, of almost 60 years, standing there. He owned several car dealerships in the area.

"I am so sorry, Jim," he said. Then he leaned in close and said, where only I could hear, "Don't worry about Jordan's car anymore. I will take care of everything." About two weeks later, I received a notice in the mail that the loan had been paid off. Thinking back on this act of kindness on that horrific day, alone on a bench in rural Scotland, I felt the emotion rising. The world was such a terrible place in so many ways, but there were still good people. It took me a few minutes to compose myself. I was still the only golfer on the course.

Finally feeling able to keep going, I teed off on the 4th. It's called Blind Piper, a 227-yard par three. The tee shot, not surprisingly, is totally blind. The green is located over a high ridge, with the correct line just to the left of a lone tall Scots pine. If the hill is carried at about 170 yards, the ball will then careen wildly down to the putting surface. A curious gong style bell, with a cast metal silhouette of a golfer mounted on top, should be struck as you start the search for the 5th tee. There are not any weak holes at Gairloch—two more are particular standouts.

At only 87 yards, from a tee perched high in the edge of the primordial forest, the 7th is like an intricate Fabergé jewel box. Over a bright purple heather covered mound, only the top of the flag is visible. The glorious golden crescent of Gairloch Beach lies beyond. To find the green, a three-quarter wedge must be perfectly judged. An dun, as it is called, deserves to be in the category of other great ultra-short holes, like the 9th at Durness and 13th at Brora.

The 8th hole, called Traigh Mor, is a 526-yard par five that would not be out of place on a major championship venue. A sharp dogleg left along the beach, at about 350 yards from the tee the fairway drops almost 50 feet vertically. Therefore, the second is completely blind—if you choose to carry the cliff. If a layup is the choice, it will leave a blind 175-yard third shot. The green is in a lovely dell, with the clubhouse situated directly on the hill beyond. This is a unique, fun, and highly strategic hole.

I could see the café was now open as I putted out on the 9th, another nice par three with the tee next to the beach. Taken altogether, the "billy-goat layout" of Gairloch came to a par of 32. I ordered tea and a sausage roll and sat by the window looking right back down the wild 8th fairway. I had planned to play a quick nine, check out of the hotel and drive on to Durness. This place deserved another round or two. A call to the front desk at the Gairloch Hotel secured my room for another night.

The second time out, there were a few golfers on the course. On the 3rd fairway, I met a confused Englishman and his wife. The pair had gone from the 4th green to the 8th tee—not realizing their mistake until they reached the 8th green. It took a few minutes, but I finally explained to them how to play the 5th hole. The routing of Gairloch is eccentric. The 5th crosses the 4th green and plays over both the 8th and 6th fairway. The 2nd hole plays across the first. The 9th plays across the 8th. It's glorious madness, and easy to get confused the first time around. I went around three times. A late reservation in the hotel restaurant provided a great end to the day. Once again, I was able to sleep for several hours.

After tea and toast the next morning, I said goodbye to Gairloch—making one last quick visit to the course to get a few more photos of the stunning 8th hole. It was still another 124 miles to Durness and meant to be a drive of three hours. The road, if possible, became even more narrow. The sky was dark and forboding. My mood started to reflect the conditions.

I reached Durness, the northernmost course in mainland Scotland, around 11 am, to find the unlocked clubhouse was deserted. My car was alone in the small car park. A nice local gentleman must have seen me drive up the narrow road to the course and came to greet me as I was walking out of the tidy but empty clubhouse. "Do you need any help?," he asked. I explained that I was actually a member, joining during the pandemic to help the club, and that I'd always wanted to play it. "Aye, there were many folks around the world that did that. It was much appreciated," he said. "Well, it's a pity about the weather. You've got it to yourself today." He then explained the entire nine-hole routing to me, which was helpful considering the first hole is a 90-degree dogleg left straight up a mountain.

The haar and thick mist of rain lent an air of mystery to this wild, remote outpost of golf. After climbing the mountain to the first green, I began to understand why Durness is beloved by so many. The view back down to the 8th and 9th holes, both hard by the Atlantic, is spectacular. I walked slowly alone among the heroic dunes, taking time to hit as many shots as I wanted.

Jordan had an original 1990s-era Scotty Cameron putter that he had used since he was 12 years old. It's identical to the one that Jordan Spieth still uses. I oiled it for him with gun metal oil before every tournament. It was the putter he used to win the state championship on that memorable day in 2015. He loved that club. I had brought it with me to use on this trip. When I reached the 5th tee, I remembered a conversation we had about Scottish courses in the weeks before he died. We watched short videos of Dunaverty, Durness, Machrihanish, and others on YouTube. He said that Durness looked like a place he would love to go.

There's a bench behind the tee looking down the wonderful 5th fairway—the entire world of Durness is spread out before you. I sat there and pulled out my son's putter. I ran my fingers across the lead tape he had carefully put on the bottom of it. I remembered the night we went to the store to buy the tape and a dozen high number Pro V1s, his favorite ball. We stopped to eat at a Buffalo Wild Wings on the way home. Parents do not realize how precious and fleeting these simple everyday moments are. "I am so sorry you are not here, baby," I said quietly to the howling wind as I held my son's favorite club. For the first time since arriving in Scotland, I sobbed uncontrollably.

I felt like screaming into the face of the gale. There was nobody within miles that would ever hear me. A cold, sideways rain started to sting against my face. For a moment, it crossed my mind that I should just lay down on the 5th tee at Durness and die. If there were reasons to keep going, they were beyond my comprehension at this moment. Mercifully, a feeling of numbness took over my brain and body. I played the 5th hole because I was here … and that was the only thing I could do.

At the 8th tee, the numbing grief started to recede. I was still a golfer after all. The stunning, downhill par four, with its green perched on the edge of the Atlantic, brought a slight smile to my face. Jordan would have loved this hole, I thought, so I should at least attempt to play it correctly. A good drive, and running chip down the hill, led to my first birdie in several days.

One great hole was followed by another. The par-three 9th hole is like a miniature, affordable, everyman version of the 16th at

Cypress Point. Waves crashed against the rocks in the cool, heavy mist as I finished my round at Durness. On the way to the car park, a hiker walked past me and said hello. The village was absolutely jammed with holiday goers: campers, cyclists, hikers, and motor bikers. There were two small cafés open for lunch, and both had throngs of people waiting to get inside. It seemed best to continue to the inn I had booked about 50 miles away in Strathy, just outside of Thurso.

11 THE NORTH REMEMBERS

*"If God meant to interfere in the degeneracy of
mankind, would he have not done so by now?"*

—The Judge, Cormac McCarthy, *Blood Meridian*

From Durness, I took the harrowing A838 around Loch Eriboll.
The camper vans heading west barreled along the narrow,
single-track road toward the oncoming cars, sometimes four
in a row, seemingly daring them to proceed. I took to pulling over
into the nearest passing place whenever I would see them coming in
the distance. If a local driver gets behind you on this stretch of road,
it's best to pull over and let them pass as quickly as possible. The
bleak, raw, natural beauty of the area offered some compensation
for the trials of the road.

It took three hours to drive 50 miles. On one of my many stops
on the verge, I called ahead to book a table for dinner. The road

suddenly (and ironically) improved just before I reached the Strathy Inn. Mentally exhausted from the drive, I dumped my bags in the room and headed straight for the bar. A bright red "T" was mounted above the barroom door. Behind the dark, intimate room was a man in his early fifties. A peat fire in the adjacent dining area put off a welcome, comforting warmth.

"I've got a table booked for 8:30."

"Mr. Hartsell?"

"That's me."

"Where have you just come in from?"

"Durness."

"You'll be wanting a drink then."

The selection of whiskies looked impressive and inviting. I ordered a pint of Tennent's and an Oban 12.

Heather and Craig Frost own and run the Strathy Inn: advertised as "a traditional inn, home cooked food, bed & breakfast." Craig was a civil servant in Devon, England for the first 10 years of his career. "That is never what I intended to do with my life. It just happened," he explained. In the early 2000s the couple started to look for an old country inn for sale in Scotland: a dream that many of us have had at one time or another. After searching for two years, they made an offer on a place on the northwest coast, but the deal fell apart when they failed to find a buyer for their house in Devon. He saw a listing for the Strathy Inn and flew to Inverness and drove north. "It was run down and needed a lot of work, but it was exactly what we were looking for," he recalls. With four bedrooms and a semi-detached public bar, it had all the elements of a traditional Scottish country inn. Fourteen years later, they were still in Strathy and far away from the daily grind of the normal world—both geographically and philosophically.

Craig Frost brought me the special of the day, a roast duck leg perfectly prepared by Heather. After the meal was finished, he came back over to talk.

"I've really loved living here and running this place, except for the last two years," he admitted. "We used to have a lot of European guests. The pandemic stopped everything. The camper vans are jamming up the roads now. You are our first American guest since the start of Covid."

He brought me another whisky before I switched to coffee. Outside of the window, sheep were grazing in a rolling field. The peat fire continued to burn. I envied the Frosts' way of life. If you have an opportunity to live out your dreams, you should take it. Time just gets away from us all.

During breakfast the next morning, I briefly considered driving back to Durness to play again. The Strathy Inn seemed like an ideal place to spend a few nights. A day trip to the west didn't seem very inviting. The links of Reay, a James Braid design, was only 15 minutes away. It's another course I had learned about from *Hell's Golfer*. I had always been curious to see it. My hastily written email to the club received an almost immediate reply: "The clubhouse is undergoing some renovations just now, but you are welcome to play. We aren't very busy today. Just put your greens fee in the box."

A pair of white building contractor vans were in the car park, but that was all. An electrician was on a ladder working on wiring above the ceiling in the bar. I put some pound notes in the honesty box near the front door and small Starter's room. A familiar feeling of excitement of discovering a new place came over me. My bag felt heavy, so I grabbed a trolley, making a mental note to put another £2 in the box when I finished.

The opening holes at Reay do not follow the typical, welcoming James Braid fashion. The 1st is 235-yard par three, unreachable into the freshening wind. The 428-yard par-four 2nd, also into the wind, did not offer a respite. At the 4th hole, called Sahara, Reay enters the realm of the dramatic and memorable. A testing par five of 581 yards, it reveals the more theatrical land of dunes and ridges. The green is situated at the base of several large sandhills and next to a tidal inlet. The last 150 yards are downhill—a running punch shot under the wind is required.

On the 2nd green, I had looked back to the clubhouse and noticed a lone golfer starting his round. By the time I reached the 5th tee, he was approaching the 4th green. It was inevitable that I was going to be overtaken. The speed at which the Scots progress around the course—while not actually rushing their game—is remarkable. I waited on the elevated tee next to the beach and waved him through.

"Aye, thank you. Lovely day, is it not? It's perfect out here with a wee bit of wind and no rain-like," he said as he teed up his ball. He hit a low, half-topped shot that ran 140 yards onto the front of the par-three green. "I'll take that one," he said with a laugh, and was gone. I never saw him again. He must've gone around Reay in less than three hours.

If Reay was located 250 miles to the south, it would be mentioned in the same breath as places like Panmure and Elie. Its remoteness places it off the radar of most touring golfers, but also adds to the aura of the experience. From the 4th hole on, it's wonderful and memorable. The par three 9th, called Chapel, is in an isolated northern corner of the course. The hole stretches along the beach. There's a bench behind the green—all you hear is the sound of a rushing burn, the ocean waves, and the wind. I don't know how long I sat there.

The inward holes flow tastefully over the rolling natural terrain, as only Braid could do. The 12th is 390 yards and called Chimneys. The approach shot is completely blind—several large brick chimneys are the aiming point. A rambling, fantastic, Georgian manor house sat behind the green. The 16th, Reay Kirk, is 314 yards and tumbles wildly downhill from the tee to the green, with the local church on the hill beyond. If I were to choose a favorite hole at Reay, this would be it. The 18th is a 152-yard par three, with an antediluvian set of gravestones almost floating behind the green. Reay would be an ideal course to play every day—5,800 yards and par 69—challenging in its way but never overbearing or oppressive.

The clubhouse was still empty: even the electrician had gone. I wanted to tell the secretary how much I had enjoyed the course. A two-pound coin in the honesty box took care of my hired trolley. This place deserved another round, but my legs were not willing. It was lunch time, so I decided to drive a few miles to Thurso. Just outside of town, there was a colorful sign for the Blue Door Café. The name seemed intriguing, so I turned down the gravel drive. The café was in a nondescript rectangular building located in the middle of a caravan park. The unassuming exterior gave way to a colorful and lively interior, decorated in the style of an old American diner. At 1:30 pm, it was filled with people. I sat at an empty table by the bright blue door.

A woman in a green Baylor University sweatshirt came over to take my order, speaking in a strong Southern accent. After over two and a half weeks in the most remote parts of Scotland, hearing that was a shock to the system. I had only seen three other Americans on the entire trip. When I spoke, she was equally surprised.

"Where are you from?"

"Alabama. I'm here for at least a month."

"I knew it was either Alabama or Mississippi! I'm from Louisiana."

She had met her Scottish husband at Baylor Law School, some 25 years earlier. On their first visit to his hometown of Thurso, she fell in love with the area and didn't want to go back. An old café in the caravan park by the beach was for sale and they bought it. She serves American style hamburgers and milkshakes—and quite successfully, by the look of the crowded dining room. We talked about college football for a few minutes: something as foreign to most Scots as shinty is to most Americans. After a nice lunch, I spent the afternoon walking around town. It didn't take long to see why Kim at the Blue Door Café had never returned to Louisiana.

After another pleasant evening at the Strathy Inn, I decided to drive to Wick Golf Club, 25 minutes southwest of Thurso. Craig Frost had mentioned that I might enjoy it. The longer way takes you through John O' Groats, the northernmost point on the UK mainland. I made an obligatory stop at the well-known signpost. A few minutes later, I walked into the Wick clubhouse. Unlike Reay, there were a few people in the bar. I was greeted by the general manager, a friendly lady named Cat.

"Hiya! What can I help you with?"

"I was hoping to play this morning."

"Aye, no bother. It's not busy. Off you go. You can pay me when you get done." She quickly returned to her work behind the bar.

Wick Golf Club was founded in 1870. The current 6,123-yard, par 69 layout dates to 1907 and was designed by Mr. John Sutherland, then the secretary at Royal Dornoch. Wick is the quintessential traditional Scottish links. It's straightforward and honest, with fiery fast-running turf. The course was delightful to play, but my game was falling apart in the wind. Golf balls were disappearing into the tall fescue rough at an alarming rate. At the lovely 151-yard 14th, Plateau, my tee shot landed just left of the green and vanished into the rough. After looking for several minutes, it was nowhere to be found. I opened my bag to get another ball and there was only one left: the old, British-size Dunlop 65 that Robbie had found in a rabbit hole on the Isle of Colonsay.

Suddenly I started to question myself. I was old and tired. *What was I doing out here at the ends of the earth? My son was gone. I could not bring him back. What was I trying to prove? What was I going to do with the time I had left?* All the energy was drained from my body. I started to walk in toward the clubhouse, something I had never done before in Scotland—even in the most violent rain and wind. Before I got past the 15th tee, I heard Jordan's voice as clear as if he was standing next to me.

"Don't quit, Dad."

It stopped me cold. Just as I had during the encounter with the deer at Ballachulish, I felt Jordan's presence. I walked back to the tee and got the old Dunlop out of my pocket. I didn't want to lose the treasure from Colonsay, but I had to keep playing. I owed it to my son. Wick deserved better.

As fate would have it, the 15th, Desert, was the number one handicap hole on the course—a long, tough par four, straight into the wind. Fearful of losing the Dunlop, I took a half swing with my driver and managed to hit the fairway. After a pair of choked down 7 iron shots, I reached the green, nearly holing a long par putt. Bogey.

The 16th hole, Cable House, is the best at Wick. The tee is benched into the side of a tall dune. I heard a low voice and looked up, almost vertically, to see a man walking his dog along the top of the ridge. The fairway sweeps to the left around the dune ridge, where the sea—the source of constant background noise the entire round—was finally visible. The green is located next to an old stone telegraph station by the bay. Energized by the bogey, I swung a little harder and hit my best drive of the day—the smaller Dunlop cutting through the wind like it was meant to do. From about 100 yards, I hit a low 8 iron that barely left the ground. It almost hit the flag and stopped two feet away. Birdie.

The 17th tee is right next to the old cable house and the sea. It's a nice hole along the bay, moving gently to the left. After another good drive, I punched another low runner and got down in two putts from just off the green. Par.

At the 18th, I pulled my drive left, but saw it bounce in the edge of the rough. If the ball bounces in the Scottish rough, there's a decent chance it will be found. If it dives in and vanishes, there's not much reason to search. The old ball was sitting up, almost like it was on a tee. It came out clean, about 30 yards short of the green—which is in front of the clubhouse. A clock on the gable wall read 12:30 exactly. After a chip to 10 feet, my last putt with the Hebridean Dunlop 65 dropped slowly over the edge of the hole. Par.

"I didn't quit, Jordan," I said quietly to myself as I replaced the flag.

Back inside the warm and cheerful clubhouse, Cat was still at her station behind the bar. I handed her my greens fee. "How did you find the course?," she asked.

"I really enjoyed it. It's a true links," I replied.

"Aye, we don't get many Americans up here, but the ones that do visit always seem to come back. I hope you will," she said.

"It would be my honor."

On the way back to Strathy, I found a small café on the main street in Thurso that was open for lunch. Walking out of the café after tea and a sandwich, I noticed the Tall Tales Bookshop across the street. A sign over the door read, "*Scorries cownin for a pucklie rain.*" I had no idea what that meant, but the rest of my afternoon was settled. A couple of hours perusing dusty old volumes yielded a nice copy of *The Long Green Fairway* by Pat Ward-Thomas.

My last evening at the Strathy Inn once again involved a night of conversation with the friendly Craig Frost. The topics ranged from Brexit and Scottish independence to life in this remote part of the Highlands—"Our phone service and internet can be hit or miss at times." I asked for his wife's rhubarb-ginger sorbet recipe. I was off to Brora in the morning.

"Don't take the coastal road," he offered. "Take the A897 at Melvich, before you get to Reay. It's a single track, but nobody will be on it in the morning. It's a lovely drive that follows the Halladale and Helmsdale Rivers—that's where Prince Charles does his fly-fishing."

On a cool morning, I turned south at Melvich. Just as advertised, it was a narrow, winding road of 40 miles through lovely countryside, with the shallow, meandering river always to my right. The sky was startlingly clear. Not due at Brora until the afternoon, I drove very slowly, taking in the scenery and stopping several times by the river. The Halladale ended at Loch an Rhuathair. The road eventually followed the path of the River Helmsdale. A lone fly fisherman was standing in the river, casting back and forth. I pulled over on the verge to watch him. There was a rhythmic beauty to the flowing arc of his line, which was highlighted by the early morning sun. If he saw me watching from a distance, he never let on.

My first and only visit to Brora had been almost 30 years earlier. I was in Dornoch with my father for a few days to play one of the world's great courses: Royal Dornoch. At breakfast one morning, our bed and breakfast host had suggested that we play Brora, a place we had never heard of. As we finished our poached eggs and toast, he booked a tee time for us. It was a wonderful day playing golf among the highland cows and sheep, which roamed freely over the links. We had never experienced anything else like it. The greens fee was £10. Brora was a welcome antidote to the beautiful difficulty of the championship links at Dornoch.

During lunch in the clubhouse, my dad, who loves Asian food, got excited when he saw a fried egg roll on the menu. He ordered two of them to go with his Diet Coke. The look on his face when the waitress returned with two rolls of bread, each enclosing a sunny-side-up fried egg, is something I will never forget. It was our first trip to Scotland. We didn't know any better.

It is much to my detriment that it had taken so long to return to play this subtle, elegant James Braid masterpiece. Malcolm Murray, who I had messaged with many times on Twitter, was coordinating a busy day in his wonderfully stocked pro shop. "You'll find that not much has changed in the last 30 years, Jim. The course is in great shape just now. We had a haar this morning, but it has mostly burned off." I walked out to the 1st tee, perched high above Brora Beach, to reacquaint myself with Braid's ethereal links.

At 297 yards, and called Ardassie, the 1st is my favorite Braid opening hole. Unlike Reay, here is the more familiar welcoming start to the day. The drive should be played well left to open up the best angle to a green that sits stately and timelessly in the dunes. The green is not visible from the tee. For all the world, it looks like it's straight ahead of you—that's actually the 17th green. On our first visit all those years ago, we were stopped by a friendly member from playing to the wrong hole. Even in 1994, he must have been used to unsuspecting Americans making this common mistake.

The 2nd, Bents, is another good hole, although there are not any weak ones at Brora. It's not overbearing at just 344 yards. The fairway temporarily runs out at about 250 yards from the beachside tee. Mere mortals will lay up, depending on the wind direction. The approach shot allows the option to either pay a traditional, low-running shot into the green or the more modern, lofted wedge. My short run of form at Reay had miraculously continued, with two pars to start at Brora. Delusions of grandeur filled my head.

The 325-yard 4th, White Post, is yet another immensely enjoyable hole. If anything, that might be the overall theme of Brora: fun. For most players, the second shot will be played blind over a ridge toward a tall white post. The green is placed just where it needs to be, with three surrounding pot bunkers, in the natural terrain. The great-grandchildren of the sheep from 1994 welcomed me back on the 9th tee, a lovely 146-yarder called the Sea Hole. My mood was much improved after the momentary crisis at Wick. It's impossible to walk around Brora and not be happy.

The links at Brora are a pure example of a classic out-and-back layout. It's 6,211 yards with a par of 70. At the 10th, you turn toward home. Now the wind, which has been a friend for nine holes, will likely become an adversary for the remaining nine. The 108-yard 13th, Snake, is another intricate jewel. A winding burn "snakes" its way between the tee and a small green guarded by five deep pot bunkers. Several large, shaggy Highland "coos" grazed by the burn, oblivious to my presence. They looked friendly, but I kept my distance, remembering how Robbie saved me from being trampled to death by another cow at Kiloran Beach.

The 345-yard 16th, Plateau, is a standout on the inward nine. With a helping wind, it's tempting to let one fly towards the green, but this is unwise. A hurting wind made the drive from the elevated tee even more difficult—anything up in the air with sidespin was likely to land in a field of grazing sheep. The approach shot is blind to an exposed green high on top of a dune. An unusual marker pole features a kite—in the shape of the Brora bird logo—tethered to the top. As the kite whipped loudly in the stiff breeze, I thought of the *Golf in the Kingdom* quote from Shivas Irons: "We are all kites in that wind." It's a unique and singular hole. From the vantage point of the green, the entire world of Brora is spread out before you. The gently rolling links give way to the beach and then the sea. Grazing sheep dot the landscape like tiny earthbound clouds.

Braid was not averse to ending a course with a par three. The finishing hole is a tough 200-yarder. It plays uphill to a green situated under the watchful gaze of the members, having tea or a pint in the upstairs bar. You cannot help but think you are being observed and discussed as you play the 18th: *What do you think he'll do with this one? It always breaks more right than you think.* Malcolm Murray was waiting in the pro shop after I finished.

"How did you get on? Did you play well?," he asked.

"For me, yes. I managed an 82," I responded.

"Aye, that's well done around here." He thanked me for my purchase of golf balls and club merchandise. The pandemic had been tough on places like Brora, which rely heavily on visitor play.

"We really appreciate all the support from the US and around the world. It saved us during the pandemic, to be honest," said the friendly Brora professional. No Laying Up, an American golf media and merchandise group, had issued a special Brora golf towel and donated all proceeds to the club. Many people around the world bought merchandise directly from the club to help keep money coming in. This outpouring of support was well-deserved. The world needs places like Brora.

I said goodbye to Malcolm. It was good to see his pro shop so busy. Upstairs at the bar, I asked for a fried egg roll and a Diet Coke. The waitress smiled a little skeptically but took my order. The table where my dad and I had lunch in 1994, by the windows overlooking the course, was empty. I sat down. That day at Brora, all those years ago, was clear in my memory. My dad was young, and I could walk 54 holes in a day. We were on our first trip to Scotland: something we had dreamed about for over 10 years. Every day was an adventure. Back at home in Alabama, my two boys were still just babies who thought their dad could do no wrong. It was five years before Jordan would even be born. The passage of time once again seemed both instantaneous and eternal.

Golf had always been the source of so much joy for our family. In many ways, the game had been our way of life. I sat in the same spot where my dad had been in 1994 and realized how lucky I'd been to have him as a father. I suddenly recalled a drive home from playing golf with him on an ancient Saturday afternoon. After falling asleep, I had woken momentarily in the golden autumn light to the sound of the Alabama game on the car radio. I looked over at my dad and everything was okay in the world.

When Jordan was young, he would often fall asleep on our way home from the course. Sometimes he would wake up for a minute and look at me and smile, maybe asking, "Where are we, Dad?," before closing his eyes again. Thinking about his last moments on earth haunted me. I hoped he had known how much I loved him. The death of a child steals the future. It takes everything.

After a few minutes, a pair of golfers reached the 18th tee. I had only eaten half of my egg roll. A table of members sitting close by offered a running commentary on their shots. Even though it had taken me decades to return, it was always somehow reassuring to know that Brora was still out there. Now I knew that this place had not changed. If you love golf, that should give you comfort. It gave me a small measure of comfort on this day.

The Golspie Inn was my base for this leg of the trip. It's not far from Brora and only five minutes from Golspie Golf Club, a course that I had never previously played. Many of my past visits had focused mainly on the west coast: Ayrshire, Argyll & Bute, and the islands. I had meant to play Golspie for years, but somehow it had never happened. The morning after my round at Brora, I was greeted outside the Golspie pro shop by Inverness resident and club treasurer, Alasdair MacDougall.

"Jim? Hello. I've been following your trip on Twitter. I saw that you were planning to play Golspie today and I wanted to come out and welcome you," he said.

My new friend gave me a brief history of the course and advice on finding my way around the unique layout. He had a friendly demeanor that made me like him immediately. A nice lady named Sheila Robertson, the club vice-president, was running the pro shop and joined in our conversation.

"You should have it pretty much to yourself today. We aren't busy. The pro is out giving a playing lesson, but that's about it just now," said Sheila, who I later learned is a multiple time Ladies Club Champion. There's a feeling at Golspie that all the members pitch in to help keep the club running. They are fiercely proud of their course.

When I tried to pay my greens fee, Alasdair spoke up: "Don't worry about that, Jim. Just enjoy yourself." I do not know this for a fact, but I'm almost sure he knew the underlying reason for my trip.

There was something about the way he talked to me that seemed to convey an empathy for what I was experiencing. Without really saying anything about it, he somehow made me feel like he understood. He walked me out to the 1st tee and pointed out the best line.

Like Brora, Golspie has a James Braid design pedigree. He was hired by the club in 1925 to consult on the then-current layout. He ultimately offered a report that contained detailed directions for modifications to every hole on the course. Most of these changes were implemented by the club, with a few exceptions. Today, Golspie is gloriously schizophrenic. The first five holes are pure links, with the sea constantly in view. Tight, springy turf allows the ball to roll unimpeded—often into high fescue rough. Of this opening salvo, the 288-yard 5th hole, called Sahara, is the standout. The smart tee shot is a mid-iron to the base of a high ridge that crosses the fairway at about 210 yards away. This leaves a blind pitch over the hill, which will run wildly down to the seaside green. It's a rolling, thrilling links golf hole.

The 6th and 7th are two transitional holes. Turning inland away from the sea, they are a hybrid of links and heathland golf. They are also two of the best holes on the course. The 6th, called Saucer, is a lovely 151-yard par three. The tee sits by the seawall and the green is set in a depression at the base of several large dunes, with the stark mountains of Beinn Lunndaidh and Beinn a' Bhragaidh looming beyond.

A statue of the 1st Duke of Sutherland, known locally as the "Mannie," sits atop Ben Bhraggie and looms over your entire round at Golspie. It was erected in 1837, after the Duke's death in 1833. The controversial figure played a key role in one of the darkest chapters in Scottish history: the Highland Clearances. Between 1811 and 1820, the Duke oversaw forced evictions of tenants from his vast Highland estate, often resorting to the use of violence. It was a terrible time. The people of Scotland have endured much, yet they have always persevered. It's possible that their suffering has made them more receptive to the pain of others. I had certainly sensed that today, even more than usual.

The 285-yard 7th hole is simply wonderful. The uphill tee shot is played to a somewhat tight fairway that's lined by gorse. A tall ridge bisects the fairway at about 240 yards, effectively making the carry more like 300 yards—most drives are almost guaranteed to end up short of the ridge, leaving a blind approach shot. Once over the ridge, the fairway is a fast ski slope down to a green surrounded by whins and native grasses. An unusual and striking triangular marker pole provides directional assistance.

From the 8th through the 11th, the course is pure heathland in character. The holes are framed by large swatches of brilliant purple heather and ball-devouring gorse. This stretch would not be out of place at Walton Heath or Gleneagles and feels the most like Braid to me. At the 12th and 13th, the course changes once again, this time to a parkland style. At the par five 14th, you return to the linksland for the remainder of the round.

Alasdair MacDougall was waiting for me on the tee of the stunning 175-yard 16th, called Cairngorms.

"What do you think of our course?," he asked.

"It's wonderful, Alasadair. Beautiful. I've never played anything quite like it. Such a great variety of holes."

"Aye. We've long been a stepchild to Dornoch and Brora, but that has finally started to change. I'm so glad you came to visit."

I was curious about his thoughts on the statue on the hill, which lorded over Golspie like an eternal ghost.

"Aye, the Mannie. Many people want to tear him down. Most of the locals think he should stay, so we will never forget what happened."

12

I HOPE YOU FIND PEACE

"And how beautiful the vacated links at dawn, when the dew gleams untrodden beneath the pendant flags and the long shadows lie quiet on the green."

—Arnold Haultain, *The Mystery of Golf* (1908)

The royal burgh of Dornoch is picturesque, even by the high standards of the Scottish countryside. It's also one of the great golf towns of the world—in the conversation with St. Andrews, Pinehurst, North Berwick, and Gullane. With no set plans for the day, a return visit to Dornoch seemed necessary. It was nice to walk down Castle Street again after so many years, with Dornoch Cathedral keeping its solemn watch over the lovely town square. I found a small café with a window table and ordered tea. On that same 1994 trip to Brora, I played a round at Royal Dornoch that I've never forgotten.

Back in those days, I would play golf until dark. Every moment of daylight in Scotland was precious. After a morning round at Dornoch and long lunch in the clubhouse, my dad was done for the day. He decided to go back to our room and rest. I walked into the pro shop to see if I could go out again. As luck would have it, there was a single golfer preparing to tee off. I hurried out to the 1st tee and found a man in his mid-sixties getting out of a golf cart. It was an old-style buggy with no roof, and the first one I had seen on the trip. I didn't think they existed in this country. He introduced himself as John from California and seemed very happy to have a partner for the round.

He played from the red tees and hit the ball dead straight. A good drive went about 200 yards. We had a wonderful time playing together. He would exclaim, "Great shot, Jim!", when I managed a good one into Dornoch's maddening greens. I was taking photos, with a real camera, on every hole. At the 10th tee, he asked me to take a picture of him with the beach and North Sea in the background. I noticed he was moving a bit slower as the round went on. On the famous par-four 14th, Foxy, he stopped on the way back to his cart.

"I have wanted to play Royal Dornoch for over 30 years. I have dreamed about it. The doctor has told me I don't have much time left. Playing with you here today has been one of the highlights of my life."

I was only 28 years old at the time. I was stunned and didn't know how to respond. We played the last few holes in relative silence. He removed his cap and shook my hand on the 18th green. "Thank you so much for the game, Jim. It was great. Would you mind sending me a copy of your photos when you get back home?" He carefully wrote down his mailing address on the back of a scorecard. He drove off. When he got out of his cart, I saw a woman hug him. She had been waiting by the clubhouse as we finished.

A few weeks later, I mailed several photos to the address in California, along with a short note. In the photo on the 10th tee, he was smiling casually like it was just a normal, everyday golf outing.

About nine months later, I had almost forgotten about it. I was a young architect with two small boys. Life was hectic. One afternoon I received a short thank you note in the mail from his wife:

Dear Jim,

John loved the photos that you sent from Royal Dornoch. That was one of the happiest days of his life. He passed away a few weeks ago. I wanted to let you know.

As I sat in this quiet Dornoch café, I remembered that round from so many years before. I had lived a lifetime since this man had died. He had lived out his dream before it was too late. It was something I had thought of frequently in the intervening years. We had met by the most random of chances—for just a few hours on a golf course—yet it had affected me greatly. That day at Dornoch might have been the last time he ever played golf. In the face of that, he was happy and enjoying every second of the experience. He wanted to see the photos. In my scrapbook of that trip, I had kept a picture of him standing on the 18th green with putter in hand. He was smiling like it was the greatest day of his life. Maybe it had been.

When I received that note, I had vowed to try to enjoy life and not put things off. That had been my overriding philosophy of life until Jordan died. It was one of the reasons I decided to go all in on my son's golf, in spite of the extreme costs and commitment that high-level junior golf entails. In the back of my mind, I had always believed that Jordan was just going through a hard time, like many young people do in the transition from childhood to the realities of the harsh world. He was trying to come back to us and just didn't make it. It was heartbreaking.

Coming back to Scotland—a place that had meant nothing but happiness to my family—was the only thing that had made any sense. In reality, I wasn't sure that I'd be able to keep going. The lack of sleep at home, and constant nightmares when I managed to doze off, had taken a toll on me. At the very least, I had to try something different. In some small ways, being in this beautiful country had helped. Here, I wanted to get out of bed every morning. That was a start. If there were any larger answers, maybe they could be found here.

My reverie was broken by the waitress asking if I needed more tea. I paid my tab and walked down to the 1st tee at Dornoch. It was a nice day, and the tee was jammed. I suddenly wanted to play more golf. With most of the day remaining to explore, I decided to drive over to Portmahomack. Jake and I had hoped to play the nine-hole course there, also known as Tarbat, in 2019. We had only made it as far north as Cullen and Covesea on that trip.

There was a lively group of golfers sitting at tables outside the Portmahomack clubhouse, enjoying the weather. Just inside the door was an honesty box. The greens fee was £20 for either 9 or 18 holes. I added an extra £3 for a trolley. A threesome was on the 1st tee preparing to tee off. It looked like a father and his sons. They saw me walk up. "Are you out by yourself?," the oldest of the group, the father, asked.

"Yes, it's just me," I replied.

"Off you go then."

Portmahomack has everything that exemplifies the uniqueness of Scottish golf—blind shots, fast-running turf, quirky holes. I played the opening hole quickly, mindful of the group that let me pass through. The 1st at Tarbat is very good: a 288-yard par four, over wildly undulating ground, with a slightly blind, depressed, semi-punchbowl green. Why did golf course architects abandon these types of holes?

The course winds through old farmland with dramatic land movement. The 6th, Seafield, is one of the best holes at Tarbat. It's 353 yards, bordered on the left by sheep-filled pastureland and on the right by a tall, fescue-covered ridge that crosses the fairway diagonally at about 250 yards from the tee. The drive for most players will land short of the hill, leaving a blind pitch over the steep rise. I dropped a ball at the top of the slope. It trickled slowly for 100 yards all the way to the front of the green.

The 8th hole is as good as the 6th. Called Jackie's Brawest, it's a 297-yard par four over wildly undulating ground. The green is perched precariously on one of the mounds and drops off steeply on all sides. It sits in front of a beautiful churchyard and old burial ground. A sign on the ancient stone wall, behind the adjacent 9th tee, reads: Amen Corner.

I took so much time photographing the 8th, I hadn't noticed an older man standing in the fairway behind me. I quickly waved him up and walked over to the 9th tee. The scene at Amen Corner was extraordinary. I thought to just let the man play through so I could take it all in for a little longer. He finished the 8th quickly and walked over. I took him to be at least in his early eighties.

"We've got the best of it today, young man. Do you want to play the last together?"

How could I refuse? He teed off first—with a short, almost non-existent backswing—and hit a low, running draw that went about 200 yards. "Well done," I said.

"Aye, not bad for an old man," he said with a smile.

"Do you play here much?," I asked, as we walked quickly down the fairway together.

"Every day that I can. It keeps me young. I love being on the golf course," he replied. After his tap in par, we shook hands. "Enjoy the rest of this lovely day," he said. I didn't even ask his name.

Back at the Golspie Inn, mussels mariniere was the nightly special. I took a pint outside and waited for my table. On the edge of the quiet garden was a tall, pyramid-shaped, wildly spiraling tree. There was an app on my phone that Jordan had sent me when he was working on the greenkeeping crew. It identifies plant species from photographs. We would use it to identify various weeds and wildflowers in our tiny backyard golf course, which I ceremoniously named after my favorite course. He thought that was so funny. I could clearly remember him putting up a sign for Royal West Dunaverty on the fence behind the green. It struck me that working on that course might've been his way of showing he still loved me. I felt a sharp stab of grief. It would be nearly impossible for me to maintain the small course as he had done.

Using the app, I learned the bizarrely beautiful tree was an *Araucaria araucana*. It's commonly called a Monkey-Puzzle Tree or Chilean Pine, native to Argentina and Chile. I stared at the twisting branches and thought about the old member at Portmahomack. He seemed to have life figured out. The server brought me another pint of Belhaven Best. I sat silently, trying to solve the mysterious puzzle of the tree. A few groups were gathered around the tables in the lovely garden. I didn't mind being alone. My last night in Golspie was a quiet one.

Earlier in the trip, Robbie had pointed out Comrie and Killin—nine-hole courses about 40 minutes apart. They were both on my way back south to the Ardrossan ferry. The drive from Golspie through the Cairngorms took about three and a half hours—a lengthy trek by Scottish standards. It included an interesting and lovely stretch of rolling hills and old churches on the A822, called the Old Military Road. It ended at the A85 near Crieff, not far from my destination. This part of Scotland is underrated for its natural beauty.

Comrie sits on a hillside just off the main road, with stunning views of the surrounding mountains of Perthshire. Unlike many places I had been on this trip, the car park was full. A women's competition was on. Unsure if I would be able to play, I inquired at the counter in the open, sunlight-filled dining room.

"The ladies will be done soon. Order some lunch and you'll be able to get off in a few minutes, no bother," came the friendly response. There were people at two of the tables, each with a large dog lying patiently at their feet.

An older lady was coming off the 9th green, with her trolley and two elderly playing partners, as I walked to the 1st tee.

"The girls are all finished now, so you'll have nothing to slow you down," she said cheerily.

"Oh, I could never keep up with Scottish lady golfers."

The happy trio found that to be humorous, but I was just being honest.

In 1921, the prolific architect James Braid was consulted on various improvements to Comrie. Those recommendations are thought to be the foundation of the current layout. The first three holes at Comrie have the feel of the assured, elegant hand of Braid. The 1st is a gentle dogleg right of 332 yards, with the second half of the fairway sloping down to a green situated next to a gigantic oak tree. It could easily have been Tolkien's model for Bilbo Baggins's party tree in *The Fellowship of the Ring*. It's a beautiful opening hole.

The 261-yard 2nd climbs uphill, through a tumbling fairway, to a green defended by two pot bunkers. A group of towering Scots pines provide a lovely backdrop. The 3rd is called Quarry: it's 158 yards and plays thrillingly uphill, over an area of rough ground, to a green perched on top of a plateau—an excellent, testing par three. The course was in pristine condition with an appealing definition between the native plant areas and fairways. Comrie was an enjoyable walk, and the clubhouse felt like the center of activity for the community. Golf in this country is part of the daily fabric of life.

When I came off the 9th green, some of the ladies from the competition were sitting under a tent outside the clubhouse. A few of them had half pint glasses of beer. I noticed the woman who had spoken to me earlier. "How did you get on?," she asked.

"Oh, it was lovely. Just lovely," I replied.

"Aye, it is. It's quite nice here," she said, before rejoining the lively conversation with her friends.

Killin Golf Club is a place I had driven past several times over the years. It was only a few minutes away from Crianlarich, where I had booked a room for the night. The sun was still shining in the early afternoon, so I decided to give it a go. A young woman was stationed behind a counter in the otherwise empty clubhouse.

"Hiya! What can I do for you?"

"I'd like to play nine holes if possible."

"Oh, aye. That's no bother at all. It will be £10. Do you need any golf balls?"

Without waiting for me to respond, she suddenly went into the adjacent room and returned with a clear plastic gallon bag full of at least 20 golf balls. She handed me the bag over the counter. Over

40 years of playing golf, and I wasn't exactly sure how to respond. "Well, how much do I owe you for these?," I asked.

"Oh, you can have them. It's all balls we found out on the course," she responded with a smile. I still have no idea why she gave me a bag of golf balls, but it was a nice gesture. I liked Killin before I even played a single hole.

Killin is a tough walk, especially if you have already hiked around one hilly course. Much like Comrie, it plays up, down, and around the side of a steep hill. The views of the surrounding mountains are arresting, and there are some very good holes. The 4th and the 5th were the two standouts for me. At 370 yards, The Gully plays over a deep depression, then up a steep ridge. The approach shot is blind. There's gorse to be avoided on the left. It's a visually striking and fun hole. Even though I was the only player on the course, I rang the signal bell loudly as I left the green. The sound echoed around the mountains of the peaceful glen. The sheep grazing in the nearby field took no notice.

The 5th, The Dyke, is only 97 yards. There's an ancient, stacked stone wall directly in front of the green—no run-up shots allowed. It's a bizarre and fun par three, the likes of which you only seem to find in the Scottish countryside. The wind had suddenly come up out of nowhere, even though the sky remained virtually free of clouds. It was impossible to hold the green with the wind directly at my back. Killin was a pleasant place to spend a late afternoon. After walking off the 9th, a dramatic downhill par five, I stuck my head in the clubhouse door to say thanks once more for the unexpected gift.

Just as I reached the Luib Hotel, traffic on the A85 came to a dead stop. I was able to drive a few yards along the grassy verge and just get into the car park. The lady proprietor was behind the bar, which was empty except for one man sipping a dram of whisky. In a few minutes, I was back downstairs in the bar. She handed me a pint of Tennent's and started a conversation.

"You are quite lucky you arrived when you did. The road is totally shut down for a motorcycle crash. It could be hours before it clears. It's almost a daily occurrence around here now. Camper vans, lorries, and motorcycles are not a good mix on these roads. The motorcycles fly around like a bat out of hell."

When I mentioned how beautiful I had found the drive down from Golspie, she got a bit philosophical.

"Aye, I've lived here my entire life. I see this countryside all the time and think nothing of it at all. Then one day I'll be out walking my wee dog down by the river and see the sun shining on the mountains and think, *this place is just stunning.* We all take too many things for granted in life."

My ferry from Ardrossan to Brodick didn't leave until 1 pm. I took advantage of the full Scottish breakfast at the Luib and made my way south on the A82 around Loch Lomond. I had driven past the town of Luss multiple times and never taken the time to stop. The small, picturesque village is made up of slate and sandstone cottages that were built for local quarry workers in the 18th century. Colorful flowers adorn the front of each building. It's one of the most popular locations in the Loch Lomond & The Trossachs National Park. It was filled with families on holiday. The car park was almost full. I walked around for a few minutes and found a bench down by the loch. Ben Lomond was reflected in the surface of the still water as if it were a mirror.

The conversation with the bartender from the previous night was still on my mind. *How many things had I taken for granted in my life? Had I taken my son for granted? Should I have encouraged him to take golf so seriously?* He had loved the game of golf. I didn't think I forced him into it. Even so, I still questioned myself. It haunted me that the pressure to succeed in golf might have been too much for him. There are so many more important things in life. Most of all, simply using the time you're given in the best way you can. Being happy. Spending time with your family. Trying to make a small difference in an increasingly difficult world. Helping other people when you can. It's possible that the day-to-day minutiae we take as given are actually the most important things. Despite what my friend said at the Luib Hotel, the Scots are much better at doing these things than most Americans. There's beauty and purpose to be found everywhere—even in the mundane—if we only take the time to look.

The ferry crossing to the Isle of Arran takes about an hour. It's one of the most traveled ferry routes in Scotland. After extricating myself from the car on the lowest deck, I walked up to the top to take in the panoramic views across the Firth of Clyde. A large basset hound was sitting upright in one of the deck chairs, just like a normal human passenger. The favorable weather of the previous three weeks continued unabated.

Just a few minutes from the Brodick ferry terminal was the Corrie Hotel, where I planned to stay for the next three nights. I got a room key from the bartender and dropped off my bags. Corrie Golf Club was just down the road. In several previous visits to Arran, I had never played Corrie. The 166-square-mile island has a population of around 4,000 people, and seven golf courses.

A small, bright-green, Victorian-looking hut serves as the clubhouse at Corrie. It was locked when I arrived. There was a sign indicating that greens fees could be paid in Fran's Tea Room, located next door. There was a ceramic bowl near the front door labeled "Burn Balls—50p Each"—some of them looked to be at least 50 years old. An old Penfold Pro caught my eye, and I grabbed it out of the bowl. A nice lady in the busy tea room, who I assume was Fran, informed me that the greens fee was £20 for a day ticket.

"I'm only playing nine."

"Just give me £10 then."

I held up the old, British-size Penfold ball. "Well, I also got this from the bowl by the door."

"Oh, just take that."

On a clear day, Corrie isn't an accurate depiction of reality. The tall, jagged peaks of Cìr Mhòr loom in the distance and look almost computer generated. The course opens with a par three, but it's at the next hole where the glorious madness begins. It's difficult to describe the 199-yard 2nd at Corrie: quirky, bizarre, beautiful, and fun are the words that immediately come to mind. For the first-time visitor, it can be hard to know how to proceed. From the tee, you see a large oak tree sitting to the left of a large mound. The number "2" is spray painted in white on the trunk. After closer study, you determine that the green is directly behind the tree. To get the ball on the putting surface, the tee shot must be played off the side of the mound, pinball style. It will then funnel down to the gathering green. It is, in my experience, a completely unique hole. Beyond the green, the stark mountains appear as avatars of some hidden paradise. I stood on the green for several minutes in stunned silence.

The layout of Corrie is sheer madness. The 1st crosses the 9th, the 3rd crosses the 7th and 8th, and the 6th crosses the 7th. The greens are in quiet clearings, on tops of ridges, or benched into sides of hills. The holes steadily progress up the hillside until the 7th tee, which is the highest point on the course. Sannox Bay shimmers in the distance. An unusual bench by the tee appeared to be carved from a whole log, almost native American, dug out canoe style. I had to sit down for a few minutes and take it all in.

In all, Corrie has five par threes and four par fours, for a par of 31. The golfers on Arran might not admit it publicly but, other than Shiskine, I think it's their favorite place to play. Like Gairloch, it rated a rare second trip around for me. The tea room was closed when I finished, so I stuck another £10 in the honesty box before I left.

An evening at the Corrie Hotel is pure entertainment. From my table in the corner by the bar, I watched people come and go almost nonstop, many of them with dogs in tow. When it got quiet—Anne, the general manager and bartender for the night—would continue our ongoing conversation about life on the island. The reliability of the CalMac ferries was a major topic. She handled the mass of customers—wanting to order drinks or takeaway fish and chips—with good-humored patience. It was quite a performance.

Shiskine Golf Club is located on the opposite side of Arran. The original nine-hole course was laid out in 1897 by Willie Fernie of Troon. The great Willie Park of Musselburgh expanded the course to 12 holes in 1912. From Colin Bannatyne's excellent centennial club history:

Willie Park's great and lasting achievement, of course, was the designing and creation of our existing 12 holes. He turned Fernie's nine inside out, retaining only two holes which we now know as Drumadoon and Kilmory (both modified in later years). Six holes on hitherto unutilized ground were created. Only a small slice of farmland was necessary for the accommodation of our two classic short holes, the Crow's Nest and the Shelf, and a further four (our 5th-8th) were fitted into the unlikely sand dune area adjacent to the point.

The B880 cuts across the middle of the island from Brodick to Blackwaterfoot, the home of Shiskine. It's a rolling, scenic drive over mountains and through farmland. The drive over from Corrie took about 30 minutes.

There are four places I must visit every time I come to Scotland: Dunaverty, Machrihanish, Prestwick, and Shiskine. These are non-negotiable for me. The collection of 12 holes on this ethereal piece of the ground is just as it should be. Dougie Bell, the Shiskine pro, was working in his well-stocked shop when I arrived on yet another nice morning. It had rained no more than two or three times in the daylight hours, and only substantially at Durness, during my entire trip. As a result, the turf at Shiskine was a gorgeous blend of yellow, brown, and light green: just how a links should look.

Dougie remembered me from my previous visit and had read some things I had written about the course. He asked after my son Jake, and we caught up on the state of the course over the previous two years. Jordan's death didn't come up, although I sensed that he knew what had happened. It's not the type of thing that's easy to bring up in casual conversation. Shiskine has a reciprocal arrangement with Dunaverty, so I only paid a nominal greens fee.

It would be easy to describe all 12 holes at Shiskine in detail. Each is a part of the intricate and wonderful puzzle that makes up the links. For me, the standouts among the 12 apostles of Shiskine are the 3rd, 4th, 6th, and 7th.

Crow's Nest, the 3rd, is 127 yards. The green is positioned high above the tee, halfway up the cliff of Drumadoon Point: a massive, striated quartz and feldspar rock formation. Of course, the tee shot is blind. A marker pole indicates the correct line, and a flag signals when the green is clear. If you are unfamiliar with Shiskine, it's easy to get confused and play toward the signal flag. There's no option but to hit a solid wedge shot just right of the marker pole—anything that comes up short is likely gone. Once you climb the hill, your reward is one of the great views in golf.

From the Crow's Nest, Shiskine is spread out below in all its rumpled, twisting, gorse-covered majesty. The shining Kilbrannan Sound and the green coast of the Kintyre Peninsula lie beyond. If you look slightly to the northeast, you might imagine that you see Carradale, a wonderful nine-hole course on the headlands above the sound. The 4th tee is just next to the 3rd green. From the heights, the tee shot on The Shelf is 147 yards down to the coast level. It's a sheer vertical drop of 75 to 100 feet and one of the most thrilling tee shots that I know of. Drumadoon Point towers over the green like the walls of a paleolithic castle.

The 6th is called the Shore Hole and is the best hole on the course. Only 274 yards, it plays alongside the beach on the right and gorse-covered dunes on the left. The fairway is a heaving affair of mounds and ridges. The green is hidden in a lovely dell at the base of large dunes with heather and gorse. Depending on the time of the year, a bright yellow or vivid purple will provide a stunning backdrop. The green can be reached from the tee. If the drive lands in just the correct spot, the ball will funnel down, and you might have a chance at an eagle two. It's among my favorite natural green sites anywhere.

Himalayas, the 173-yard 7th, is yet another blind par three. The tee shot must be played over the corner of the same dune that provides the backdrop for the stunning 6th green. The green is hidden in a quiet dell among the tall dunes. The only thing I could hear on this morning was the sound of the waves breaking on the nearby beach. An intricate and unusual system, involving a pulley rope running underground between two signal arms, is used to indicate when the green is clear. Taken all together, Shiskine has seven par threes, four par fours and one par five, for a par of 21-21-42. There's a wonderful symmetry to the "front six" and the "back six."

The course had not been crowded. I took my time walking around. Dougie was still alone in his shop.

"How did you get on, Jim? It's a perfect day to be out, is it not?"

We talked about the lovely, dry conditions and some of the stories I had written on Scotland. I mentioned that I hoped to stop by again in a few days on my way to Prestwick. As I was on my way out the door, he asked, "Would you change anything about this place, Jim?"

I stopped to reply. "If you guys ever change a single thing about this golf course, I'm calling the police."

It was still before noon, and just down the road was a nine-hole course called Machrie Bay. I had driven past (and through) the course several times but had never been able to play it. On Jake's first trip to Arran in 2019, he excitedly exclaimed, "Look Dad, somebody built a practice green down by the beach!" as we drove through the club's unusual 9th hole.

A remarkable match occurred at the small, largely unknown course 85 years before my visit. On August 10, 1937, the black Rolls-Royce driving, legendary four-time Open Champion Walter Hagen and his longtime traveling exhibition partner, Australian professional Joe Kirkwood, arrived on the west coast of Arran. The Rolls pulled up to the bucolic Machrie Bay Golf Club for their scheduled exhibition match with two local lads. Fourteen years later in 1951, the great S.L. McKinlay wrote an account of that day in the Glasgow *Herald*:

> It was a perfect afternoon. The Kintyre hills were purple, the Kilbrannan Sound was that beautiful shade of blue just darker than the sky, and the Machrie course was lush, of which latter amenity the sheep and cows were taking full advantage. Fences, of course, kept these animals from soiling the greens, but did not prevent the rabbits from happily skipping around and making little scrapes.

Not much else is known about the details of the Hagen-Kirkwood four-ball match. The names of their local competitors have been lost to the mists of time. It was reported that the local lads were 1 UP after the opening nine holes, before Hagen played the second nine in a brilliant 30 strokes, resulting in a 3 & 1 triumph by the visitors. According to a news report of the day, Hagen and Kirkwood seemed to take it all in stride—making jokes with their opponents and to the large, hastily assembled crowd of locals.

On what was to be Hagen's last trip to the United Kingdom, his traveling exhibition had gone to largely unknown Machrie Bay by mistake. Hagen had been advised by an American friend to be sure to visit Machrie on this exhibition tour—but his friend actually meant the much more celebrated Machrie Golf Club on the Isle of Islay. A beloved figure in Scotland, "Sir Walter" was the first American-born Open winner, in 1922 at Royal St. George's and also at Muirfield in 1929—and an astonishing 11 major championships overall. Joe Kirkwood was regarded as the greatest trick-shot artist of the era and a great professional himself, having won the Australian, Canadian, and North & South Opens. He competed several times in the Open Championship. It somehow seems appropriate that The Haig, who did much to break down certain class barriers in professional golf, played one of his final rounds in Scotland at a simple, nine-hole, community golf course like Machrie Bay.

The inviting Machrie Bay Tea Room serves as the de facto clubhouse and a community gathering place. Like at Corrie, the £10 greens fee here is paid at the counter. I found a trolley and started walking toward what appeared to be the only obvious (and visible) path to a golf course.

Most Scottish greenskeepers seem to have a sixth sense for recognizing lost American golfers. Walking in exactly the wrong direction, I was greeted warmly by a man pushing a lawnmower.

"Is this the way to the first tee?," I asked.

"No, no. There's a wee path behind the tea room. Walk back around there to the left, and you'll not miss it," replied David Jefferies, as he gestured toward the small building.

Jefferies is the sole caretaker of Machrie Bay. After introducing himself, he explained how to get to the 2nd tee from the 1st green, which turned out to be very useful information: "You can either walk around to the left or right of the white house behind the green," he said, "the path to the left may be a bit better just now. You'll have no problems getting around after the 2nd. I'll see you out on the course."

The path itself to the 1st tee was wonderful—sandy, narrow, and winding through gorse, bracken, and other native plants—and it created a sense of anticipation for what was to come. After emerging from the dense vegetation, a prominent sign on the tee announces, somewhat sternly:

MBGC
HAVE YOU PAID YOUR GREENS FEES?
HONESTY BOX ON HALL DOOR.

Machrie Bay starts off brilliantly. The 1st hole, named Kilbrannan, is one of the best on the course. On this 303-yard par four, one can almost imagine the great Hagen peering out into the haar, trying to discern the line for his tee shot. It's semi-blind, with a massive patch of gorse and native plants on the left, and more rough ground down the entire right side. The Kilbrannan Sound—in all its glory on this clear day—is visible from the elevated tee, and it reveals itself once again when the gorse ends on the right. The 1st green is a one-off: carved directly into the side of a small dune, it allows the approach shot to be banked off an almost vertical wall of turf and back onto the green: sheer madness of the kind seemingly found solely on the west coast of Scotland. The view back over the green and down the 1st fairway, with the Sound beyond, has to be one of the best in golf. Following David Jefferies' instructions, I took the winding path to the left around the lovely white cottage situated directly in the route to the 2nd hole. As often happens when I am in this country, I felt a brief moment of jealousy for whoever lived in such a perfect spot. The path winds through flowering native plants before arriving at the tee. The 2nd hole, named the Hummocks, is another great one. A 170-yard par three, it plays over bracken and heather-covered mounds to a hidden green, with the majestic mountains of Arran in the distance.

After the triumph of this opening pair, things become a bit more prosaic, but no less fun. The ground is suddenly a bit flatter, and the next four holes—a par three, par four, par three, and a par four respectively—are challenging and pleasant. The 4th offers the most unique hazard of this group, with a long, rough-covered mound situated about 15 yards in front of the green. It's very unusual, as it staunchly defends the green against my favorite links shot: the low-running 8 iron that never gets more than a foot off the ground. The 6th, called The Glaik, is a fun 280-yard par four with a road along the right, leading to a wonderfully sited green.

As I approached the 6th green, I saw the only other golfers on the course that morning. Teeing off on the 7th, which runs directly parallel to the 6th, was a foursome consisting of three girls and their dad, with their mother dutifully carrying the scorecard. I slowed down to watch them tee off, not wanting to catch up and rudely play through their game as a single. The two older girls appeared to be in their teens and had perfect golf swings—much better than their dad's, it must be said. The youngest was around eight years old and not advancing the ball very well, but smiling like only an eight-year-old can, who is playing golf with their dad on a perfect summer day.

The last time I played golf with all three of my boys was in late August 2019. Jordan had decided to give college golf another try and was to start classes in a week. Sweetens Cove was recovering from a flood, so we went to Sewanee, a nine-hole mountaintop course in south Tennessee. It was a great day. Jordan shot 33. Jake and Jonathan hit several good shots. Jordan took a photo of the four of us standing on the edge of the cliff behind the 4th green, with the Appalachian mountains and clear blue sky beyond. He was wearing a Country Club of Birmingham hat I had given him just a few days earlier. After the round, we went to a local hole in the wall bar called Shenanigans and ate cheeseburgers. We were all happy. This was how I had hoped to spend the rest of my life. When my time was up, maybe at age 90, my boys would take my ashes to Dunaverty

Beach… but the world doesn't work that way. This becomes a brutal reality when you lose a child.

I stood silently as the girls and their dad teed off, then turned to watch their next shots. It struck me that I was watching the essence of Scottish golf right before me: a family on holiday, walking around a beautiful golf course on a sunny day. Feeling confident that they were now far enough ahead of my pace, I finished the hole and found David Jefferies waiting for me on the 9th tee, which sits directly behind the 6th green. He turned off his mower and greeted me warmly, "How are you getting on?"

"It's wonderful," I replied, "I love it."

We stood there and talked for several minutes. I learned that David was once the club champion at Corrie and had finished high in the standings at Shiskine over the years, until back issues started to affect his game.

"I still play as much as I can, but I never know how my back will hold up. Everyone talks about Shiskine, but Corrie from the medal tees is quite challenging," he told me, almost confidentially. He mentioned his son proudly, who is a golf course superintendent at an exclusive private club in Connecticut. "Imagine him with a staff of 20, and here I am taking care of this place all by myself," he said with a laugh.

I have had many pleasant conversations with Scottish greenskeepers over the years, and this one was no exception.

"We don't get many Americans here. What brought you out today?"

I mentioned my long-time interest in the infamous Walter Hagen match, but then got to the real reason why I was spending a precious Scottish morning at Machrie Bay. "This is the kind of golf that I love the most," I said, gesturing toward the 9th fairway and the impossibly blue water beyond.

"Aye," said David Jefferies, "this is the true game." Then, as if suddenly waking from a reverie, he said, "well, that's me. It's time for tea. Enjoy the rest of your day." He walked off quickly toward the tea room and was gone.

I admit to being partial to quirky holes. The Isle of Arran has its fair share of them. The 9th, the Road Hole, a 246-yard par four, deserves a spot in the pantheon of the unusual. From an elevated tee, the fairway tumbles wildly down for about 170 yards to a hedge of heather and gorse: the boundary of the A841. This is a heavily traveled road, filled with people just off the Lochranza ferry on their way to Blackwaterfoot or Brodick. The green sits on a narrow strip of land between the road and the ocean.

Standing on the 9th tee, you might be tempted to drive over the road and onto the green. There's just no way that a ball traveling from the heights of that tee would ever stop on that putting surface. Even a perfectly struck drive would finish up on the beach or in the water. You are left with no option but to hit a 7 or 8 iron off the tee, in order to lay up at the end of the fairway. This leaves a semi-blind, 60-yard pitch that must be timed to avoid the traffic on the A841. Fortunately, you can hear the cars approaching in the distance, which helps you judge when to hit the ball. I actually started laughing when I had to wait for a few cars to pass, before I could hit my approach. Holes like this are embraced and celebrated in Scotland like nowhere else in the world.

That night I was sitting on the patio in the Brodick Bar, nursing a pint and watching dogs walk by, when I got a message on Instagram from Greg McCrae, a native of Arran and then the owner of a local wonderful small pizza and ice cream restaurant in Brodick. He saw I was in town, and a few minutes later, walked into the bar carrying his golf bag over his shoulder. Brodick Golf Club, where Greg is a member, is about a mile down the road. He walks there from his house on the hill above town.

We talked for several minutes about golf on the island, and the intricacies of pizza and ice cream on a remote rock. He asked me about the other courses I had played on my trip. Corrie was of special interest, and he seemed pleased that I had enjoyed it so much. A young girl on horseback rode past the bar. People came and went, greeting each other as only islanders who know everyone can. Greg brought us another pint. When I started to explain the reason I was there, he stopped me. "Aye, I know why you are here, Jim. I hope you find some peace."

13

WHEN REVELATION COMES

"On those ecstatic occasions, when revelation comes, you give thanks to your Creator not only for giving you life but also for giving you life as a golfer."
—Angus MacVicar, *Golf in My Gallowses*

I left the Corrie Hotel well before breakfast to catch the 8:15 ferry from Lochranza to Claonaig. There had been ongoing issues with the Brodick to Ardrossan crossing, so I had a feeling the queue might form early. It's a drive-up ferry with no bookings and the only other option to get off the island. There was only one other car in line when I arrived after the 20-minute drive, but my decision to arrive early proved to be the correct one. Across the road was a small coffee shop, no more than a hut really. Twenty years earlier, on the trip with my dad, Charles, and Chris, we had ordered hot chocolate there on a windy, cold morning on our way to Machrihanish. Jordan had been almost two years old when we made that trip. I brought a small St Andrews cap back for him, which he wore religiously for two or three years while taking wild swings at plastic golf balls in our backyard.

By the time I finished my tea and bacon roll, the queue across the road was almost full of camper vans and large motor homes. My tee time with Robbie, and Ari Techner—a friend from Sweetens Cove who now lived in Campbeltown—wasn't until 2 pm. I was excited to see Robbie again and have some company after playing so much solo golf. The Sea Captain's House, a lovely, converted 1860s lifeboat station at Dunaverty Rock, was booked for the next three nights. I invited Robbie to stay with me. It was located only about 75 yards from the 4th green at Dunaverty.

The small CalMac ferry moved over the water effortlessly across the smooth Kilbrannan Sound during the 30-minute crossing. I stood on the south side of the deck and took in the view of the narrow channel between Arran and Kintyre. There are two routes from Claonaig to Campbeltown. The main route is the A83 down the west coast of the narrow peninsula, along the Atlantic Ocean. A second option is to take the B842 along the east coast, through Carradale. It's the shorter and more direct route, but the longer drive due to the narrow, single-track road.

It's widely assumed and accepted that Paul McCartney wrote The Beatles classic "The Long and Winding Road" after a trip down the A83. In fact, the song was inspired by a drive down the other way: on the B842 to his High Park Farm outside of Campbeltown. Robbie knew the driver that had chauffeured the great man, who confirmed this story. The B842 is not quite as long as the A83, but it's definitely more winding.

My motive for taking the long and winding road this morning was simple: the B842 passes by Carradale Golf Club. Jake and I had spent a memorable day there in May 2019. I felt a strong need to see it again. It almost seemed disrespectful to be so close and not stop by.

It was around 9:30 when I reached the small, empty car park. A sign on the clubhouse wall indicated that nine holes was still just £15 and a day ticket was only £25. Using a pitching wedge as a walking stick, I went through the gate and started up the steep hill on the 1st hole, a 162-yard semi-blind par three. My destination was the 2nd tee, and a stunning 341-yard par four called Kilbrannan that cascades downhill over an old stone wall. The green sits atop a series of eccentric mounds, with the water below. I stood silently for a moment and took in the view. In the distance, the tall peak of Beinn Bharrain on Arran towered over the narrow, sparkling Sound. Jake had been so happy that day, exclaiming, "Wow, look at this dad!" when we reached the 2nd tee. It was 3 am in Alabama, but I texted him a photo. I wrote that I loved him and wished he was here with me. Robert Strang, the longtime Carradale greenkeeper, was on his mower in the distance by the 3rd green.

At the Tesco in Campbeltown, I stopped for groceries. I had the idea I would cook dinner that night at the Sea Captain's House. Trying to think of something that Robbie might enjoy, I decided on Shepherd's Pie—placing leeks, minced beef, and a couple of packs of Tennent's into my cart. Southend was only 15 minutes away. Donnie MacLean, Southend resident and owner of the group of small historic buildings on Dunaverty Rock, was standing outside when I arrived. He had lovingly converted an old lifeboat station house and small keeper's cottage into rental properties. The wooden boat-house on the point served as his workshop. The elaborate Victorian structures were beautifully restored and well-preserved. Donnie obviously took a lot of pride in his work.

"You must be, Jim!" the outgoing, and immediately likable, Scot exclaimed as I got out of my car. He was full of questions about my trip. I mentioned being an architect and how I had always been fascinated by the stately old Keil Hotel, visible across the bay. He suddenly became even more animated, "Oh, I've taken that on! I bought it a few years ago and put a roof on it and replaced the windows. It was such a pitiful mess. I don't know if I can ever do anything with it, but I've stopped it from falling in, which was important to do."

"If you ever need an architect, I'd work on it for free," I said with a laugh.

"I might take you up on that offer. I just might indeed," he replied.

The conversation turned to our families. His grandchildren were running around a tiny, enclosed garden, under a washing line with drying sheets. Donnie had a son in Campbeltown. "Do you have any children?," he asked.

I had come to dread this question. It was hard to know exactly how to answer, but I knew that even though he was somehow gone, Jordan would always be my son. I responded quietly: "Yes, I had three boys. My youngest son Jordan passed away suddenly about 10 weeks ago. He was 21."

"Oh dear, this is so terrible. Oh no, no, you poor man," he replied, hugging me tightly. I noticed that tears had formed in his eyes as he pulled away. "What happened to your wee boy? Oh, this is just so awful," he continued.

I could feel his genuine empathy, so I recounted the entire horrible story as we stood on the rocks of Dunaverty Bay. The sound of the wind and the waves providing a solemn, dirge-like soundtrack to my awful tale. He listened silently, his eyes never leaving mine, with an occasional tear streaming down his face. I am certain I told him things that I'd never talked about to anyone back home. In a strange way, it was a relief to unburden myself of this story to a man I had just met. When I finished, he put a hand on my shoulder and said, "If you need anything at all while you are here—anything—just call me. Here is my mobile number."

Robbie and Ari were already sitting at a table in the Dunaverty clubhouse. Rona was on duty at the counter. I ordered a chicken and cheese toastie, adding jokingly, "It better be as good as your sister's." I then joined my playing partners for lunch. We talked about my travels around the country. I had gone to places that Robbie had never even been.

"What's been your favorite so far, Jim?," Robbie asked, "other than Dunaverty, of course." It was a difficult question.

"I don't know," I replied. "I want to say Isle of Colonsay, but Gairloch and Durness were so good. I loved Reay. Then there is Brora and Golspie. Panmure. I don't think I can answer."

It took us around three hours to walk around the links of Dunaverty. The afternoon sun was warm and bright, but it was 65 degrees with a pleasant breeze. We had a wonderfully casual game, each of us provided with a highlight to remember. Robbie birdied the difficult par three 8th. I made birdie on the 9th, with a wind-aided drive carrying the hill and running down to the punch-bowl green. Ari birdied the 11th, which was well done into the freshening wind. The sun got lower, and brighter, on the horizon. By the time we reached the 17th tee, the fairway was illuminated in a yellow-gold light. A deer stood motionless in the rough by the bright blue Coniegien River. It was good to be alive and with friends on the golf course.

Back at the Sea Captains House, we found pint glasses for the Tennent's. I started preparations for dinner, soon realizing a major shopping error. A key ingredient of Shepherd's Pie is potatoes, which I had not purchased. The Tesco was 30 minutes away, and we had already started on our pints. Donnie was still working outside the small cottage, so I walked out on the front deck. "Donnie, this may seem like an odd request, but do you happen to have any potatoes?

He looked up and said, "I think I just might, Jim. Hang on." He came out of his shop a minute later with a sack of potatoes, just the right amount for my pie. "Here you go. Enjoy your cooking!" He went back to his work.

The kitchen/dining area in The Sea Captain's house opens onto a small deck that is seemingly cantilevered into the side of Dunaverty Rock. My shepherd's pie now safely in the oven, Robbie and I sat outside. He gave me the bloody, tragic history of Dunaverty Castle, as we looked straight up at the mighty rock. "The castle would have sat on top, just there," he said, pointing up. Daisies and green bracken ferns carpeted the hidden cove. We ate our dinner a few minutes later. An orange-red sunset over the bay was the evening's entertainment.

The next morning, we had tea and a sausage roll in the Dunaverty clubhouse. Robbie called ahead, so Rona would have it ready when we arrived. We were entered in the McKinven & Colville Better Ball Open at 1 pm at Machrihanish, Robbie's home club. I had been a member at Machrihanish from 1995 to 2010, with David Baxter of Ardell House signing my membership application. It was close second to Dunaverty on my list of personal favorites. This would not be my first "Open" at Machrihanish, as I had played in the club's Jimmy Kerr Open several times in the past.

Machrihanish Golf Club was founded in 1876. Charles Hunter of Prestwick laid out the original 12 holes. Old Tom Morris was called in to expand the links to 18 holes in 1879, after the club obtained additional linksland west of the Machrihanish River. Famously, Old Tom is said to have proclaimed (adjusted for modern day English) that the links "had been specially designed by the Almighty for playing golf." It's hard to argue with the great man's assessment.

The course began its initial run of popularity in the early 1900s when the Campbeltown and Machrihanish Light Railway opened in August 1906. The railway was an extension of the old coal mine railway from Drumlemble. It was intended to carry the large number of holiday passengers traveling to Campbeltown from the Glasgow area, via paddle steamer. The rail line ran from the Campbeltown Pier to the old Pans Hotel and 1st tee of Machrihanish Golf Club. Within three weeks of opening, over 10,000 passengers had used the rail service. It was successful for many years, with interruptions caused only by World War I.

Campbeltown Coal Company ceased operations in 1929, leaving the passenger service as the railway's sole source of income. A local bus service further eroded the need for the railway, and it closed for good in 1931. It's easy to think that adventurous golfers of today would love nothing more than to take the train from Campbeltown to the 1st tee at Machrihanish—walking down to the station from the Ardshiel Hotel with golf bags thrown over their shoulders. It was a romantic time for the area that has been largely forgotten today.

I had first visited Machrihanish with my dad on that memorable trip in 1994. A day ticket was only £18. Ken Campbell, the long-time pro, allowed us to go out as much as we wanted. We stayed at Ardell House with David Baxter for almost a week, playing golf until we were worn out, followed by dinner in the simple, unassuming clubhouse. The large bay windows in the dark, wood-paneled bar featured the sunset over the Atlantic on a nightly basis.

A large group of golfers were gathered outside the small detached pro shop, adjacent to the 1st tee. To the right of the famous tee, a granite monument announces, "Best Opening Hole of Golf in the World." It's a bold claim, but not one without merit. The tee shot is played over the Atlantic and beach, to a fairway that hugs the coastline. It is beautiful, unforgettable, and dramatic.

Open competitions in Scotland are just that: open to anyone with an established handicap willing to pay the nominal entry fee. They are a great, affordable way for golfers to experience different courses around the country. We were paired with Peter and Graham from Balmore Golf Club, north of Glasgow. It was their first trip to Machrihanish and they were excited to be here. "We try to play in two or three of these Opens a year. It's such a great way to see the country and meet people," said Graham, who was wearing a light blue Jacksonville Jaguars cap. He explained, "I just love American football."

With seemingly the entire west coast of Scotland watching us tee off, I proceeded to pull-hook my drive onto Machrihanish Beach—narrowly missing a hand-holding couple out for a Saturday afternoon stroll with their dog. "Unlucky, Jim. You'll get it there. I can see it," Robbie said sympathetically. He then proceeded to hit a low draw that ran for 75 yards down the left center of the fairway. I had a decent lie on the beach, just far enough away from some large boulders. A surprisingly well-struck 7 iron got me back in the fairway, and I salvaged a bogey—a net par for the team with my handicap. The opening hole at Machrihanish gets all the attention, but the essence of this ethereal links, for me, is the stretch of holes from the 3rd to the 8th. It's one of the most memorable runs of true links holes in golf.

The 3rd, Islay, elegantly starts this six-hole symphony of natural wonder. It's 361 yards with a blind tee shot played over the 2nd and 16th greens. A good drive, avoiding the fairway bunkers on the right, will leave a short iron into a sloping green protected by round, deep sand pits. The green is just where it should be: among the low dunes, with the hills of the Isle of Jura providing a stunning backdrop. On a sunny day, this view might be the ideal depiction of pure links golf.

The 4th, Jura, continues to build toward a crescendo. At 121 yards, it's normally a pitching wedge or 9 iron, depending on the direction of the ever-present wind. It plays over rough, tumbling, low dunes to a slightly elevated green in the ever-growing natural sandhills. A deep bunker guards the front left. It's a rare hole that is more difficult with a helping wind.

The short par-four 5th and even shorter par-four 6th, Punchbowl and Balaclava, are partners in crime. The precious linksland becomes even more turbulent and wild. The drives on both holes are played into impossibly undulating fairways. The turf at Machrihanish—as much as any course I've played—has that hollow, thumping links sound when struck with a club. It's resilient and bouncy. There are hidden bunkers and deep depressions of high rough to be avoided. The 5th green gathers shots in from the back left, but otherwise it drops off precipitously on the front and right side. At 288 yards, the 6th is a classic, short par four. With the wind, even an average player might come close to reaching the slightly concave green. In fairness, the green at Balaclava is more gathering than its curiously named predecessor. Both holes are the essence of fun.

The 420-yard 7th hole, Bruach More, ranks among the top blind holes in links golf. A massive dune ridge crosses the fairway at about 270 yards from the tee. It can't be carried from the tee, even by the ridiculous standards of today's driving distances. The approach shot is played blind over the high ridge, with only a marker pole as your guide. Once over the crest, the ball will run wildly down to the green. This hole used to have one of the natural wonders of the world of golf: a massive, natural blow-out bunker in the right-hand side of the dune ridge. It's enormous and visually stunning. According to

Robbie, it had been grassed over at some point in the 2010s, because it became too hard to maintain during the violent winter winds. I hope the club will consider restoring it someday.

The 8th hole, Gigha, is the apex of this remarkable stretch of golf. The tee shot is reminiscent of the wildness of Punchbowl and Balaclava. You are not quite sure of the best line among all the heaving dunes, but the fairway is out there somewhere. The approach is one of the most enjoyable on the course, with the green perched high on top of the dunes. It's completely exposed to the ever-present Machrihanish wind. Like the 4th, it's very difficult to judge the shot into the green, with a helping wind. If the approach falls short, the ball is likely to roll back at least 50 yards down the slope.

Thankfully I played reasonable golf, helping Robbie on several holes. I had wanted to play well for my friend at his beloved links. At the long par-five 12th, I made a 25-foot putt for birdie: a net eagle with my stroke. Robbie, not normally given to displays of emotion on the course, gave me a fist bump. "That's the Jim Hartsell I remember," he said with a smile.

We walked along briskly for the last few holes. Dark clouds had rolled in, and the wind suddenly intensified. "It's going to rain in about an hour," Robbie said with assured certainty. There was an effortless, ongoing conversation with playing partners Peter and Graham. Where else but golf can you become friends with someone after just three or four hours together? We shook hands on the 18th and signed our scorecards. I put my arm around Robbie briefly. "Thanks for the game," I said.

"No bother, Jim. You played well today." We weren't going to win the McKinven & Colville Better Ball Open, but we played solid golf. That meant more to me than I cared to admit.

A young man with a classic, fluid swing was teeing off on the 1st, silhouetted against the Atlantic. He reminded me vaguely of Jordan, and I suddenly felt my stomach roll. Like that St. Andrews cap when he was a little boy, I had brought him back a Machrihanish putter cover in 2019. He used it for the last two years of his life. When I was finally able to look in his room a few days after the funeral, his golf bag was placed neatly in the corner, everything in place. The black and white putter cover, with the club's oystercatcher logo, was still on his old Scotty Cameron.

Many of my happiest days had been spent in this special place—so many rounds over the years that I had played with my dad, Jake, Charles, Chris, and Robbie. I thought about the wonderful long evenings over dinner in the old clubhouse. I remembered the kindness that Mr. Baxter had shown to all of us. The title for my first book, *The Secret Home of Golf*, was inspired by this hidden mecca. The following is an excerpt from the poem, "Machrihanish," written by unknown author in 1883:

> When round the social board we meet,
> For golfers a' are clannish,
> We pass the night in mirth and glee,
> In the inn at Machrihanish.
> Then golfers a' tak' my advice,
> If care you want to banish,
> Tak' up you clubs, an' wi' a friend
> Set off to Machrihanish.

Robbie and I stopped at the Tesco on the way back to Dunaverty Rock, grabbing some frozen pizzas and a couple of bottles of wine. That night we sat in the high-ceilinged den of Donnie MacLean's lifeboat station. The Keil Hotel, across the bay, was centered directly on the large windows. Robbie started to open up a bit about a few things in his life that he had been worried about. We didn't talk too much about my situation, which was a relief. It was good to be there for my friend.

Before going to bed we agreed to play Dunaverty together once more in the morning. Robbie outlined the plan: "Let's just walk out to the 5th tee and start there. Nobody will be out that early on Sunday. We can stop at the clubhouse and have lunch and then play the last four holes. We'll finish up right back here at the house."

It was eerily quiet that morning. Normally you can hear the waves crashing, the ever-present howling wind or the constant braying of sheep in the distance. As we stood on the 5th tee, it was silent and calm. We were the only golfers out on the course, and we didn't say anything to each other before we teed off. We both started off hitting the ball well, but I missed short putts on the first four holes. "Unlucky, Jim," Robbie said, as I missed yet another four-footer for par on the 8th. Then he stopped. Robbie is a brilliant golfer but he rarely, if ever, gives playing advice on the course. "The only thing that matters is hitting the ball in the middle of the putter face, Jim. That is the only way you will ever make a putt. That's all there is to it."

After I failed to birdie the 9th, which was suddenly playing straight downwind, Robbie gave another rare pronouncement.

"You cannot force a birdie in links golf, Jim. You have to play for pars, and if you happen to make a birdie, that's just a bonus."

In all the golf we had played together over the past month, I had never seen him like this. He knew the pain I had been experiencing. We had talked about it some, but just in passing. I think he may have sensed that there was something different about the round this morning. Our usual jokes over errant shots and missed putts were absent. We had become close friends and were about to say goodbye. We had no idea if we would ever see each other again. Nobody ever does. I had watched Jordan cutting the grass in my backyard, probably listening to The Beatles on his headphones, and then he was gone. That may have been part of the reason for my friend's suddenly reflective mood. There was also a palpable feeling in the air. The preternatural silence continued as we played the 10th hole. It was as if someone, maybe Angus MacVicar's Creator, had turned down the volume of the earth. The strangely silent wind had completely shifted again, in the opposite direction.

The 11th tee at Dunaverty is the highest point on the course and is appropriately named Mount Zion. If there is a holy place in the game for me, this is it. There's a bench where I usually stop and sit on for as long as I feel like it. Here, the turbulent and unparalleled linksland of Dunaverty spreads out before you—with the impossibly blue Irish Sea in the far middle ground—and the coast of Northern Ireland just visible in the distance. After we both drove the green situated well below, with a helping wind I must admit, Robbie asked if we should sit for a few minutes.

The weight of everything that had happened this summer suddenly came crashing down on me. I thought about Jordan, and how much he would love hitting off this tee. He would hit his 2 iron, I thought, and I could just see him striking it with that piercing, beautiful ball flight. I thought of my son Jake, who had laughed out loud when we crested the ridge on the blind 9th hole and saw his ball on the green here just two years ago. I thought about my oldest boy Jonathan, who has his own young son. They had been so affected by their brother's death. I thought about my sweet dad, who had first come to Dunaverty with me in 1994 and loved it so much, who was still so heartbroken over the loss of his precious grandson who he had helped teach the game. I was crying and couldn't stop.

This is when the revelation came. It suddenly became clear to me that I had to keep going for Jonathan and Jake, for my new grandson Otis, for my dad, for my wife. Grief is a solitary pursuit, but only family can comprehend the sheer magnitude and pain of the loss. They still needed me, and that should be enough. I had to keep going to try to help other people learn from this senseless tragedy. Maybe there was some small way I could reach a parent who was unsure about their child being prescribed dangerous, mind-altering drugs. Maybe there was something I could do to help raise money for kids to have a chance to play the game Jordan had loved so much. I had to reclaim the memories of my son. They were not suddenly invalid and wrong because he was gone.

My time in Scotland, with people like Robbie, Alasdair MacDougall, Greg McCrae, and Donnie MacLean, had helped me understand that it was okay to grieve, but you had to find a way to continue. The Scottish sense of practicality, hard-earned through a history of suffering, demanded that. The Scottish sense of empathy and quiet understanding, earned in the same fashion, had helped me find a way to keep living.

"I'm sorry, Robbie. I'm thinking about Jordan and Jake and—."
I could not get any other words out.

Robbie put his hand on my shoulder and said, "I know, Jim. I know. God bless your soul."

My friend had to leave after our round to get back home to Lochgilphead. We stood on the deck outside of Dunaverty Rock and said our goodbyes. I started to cry again as he hugged me.

"Jim, I just want you to know that the last few weeks with you have been some of the best times of my life. You are a good person. I am so sorry for what happened with Jordan. Don't worry, I'll see you here again. You stay well my friend."

I could not get any coherent words out. My friend drove off behind the 4th green and was gone.

⟜⟶

In those first days following Jordan's death, I was reaching out for anything to grab onto. Scottish author and Shetland Islands resident Tom Morton, whose classic *Hell's Golfer* had been one of my bibles for the wilds of Scottish golf, had recently written a book titled *It Tolls for Thee,* about "reclaiming and celebrating the end of life." We had corresponded a few times on Twitter, so one night I messaged Tom with the terrible news and asked if his research for the new book had led to any revelations about how to deal with such a tragic loss. He responded immediately: "Oh Jim, I'm so sorry. I have been in Ayrshire for the past 10 days with my father, who just died on Saturday. The book ends with a quote I have found helpful and is often wrongly attributed to Queen Elizabeth: *'The pain of grief is just as much a part of life as the joy of love. It is perhaps the price we pay for love, the cost of commitment.'* I'm afraid I have no overarching insight except to say that love endures."

When you become a parent, you only have one job for the rest of your life: to protect your child. It's the only thing that really matters. I have no overarching insight to offer other than that. The revelation on Mt. Zion had also shown me that I had tried to protect Jordan as best as I possibly could. As parents, we can only do so much in this world. I had to forgive myself in order to continue. My other sons might still need me.

You might be thinking that this kind of insight would be obvious, or always present, but it's not. Far from it. When you go through crushing loss, nothing makes sense. You forget everything else. You fail to see what's around you, hiding in plain sight. The world is noise—nothing you hear makes sense. You live in your head, you clutch at your broken heart. You imagine things that are not real. At times, you aren't sure if you are conscious or in a vivid nightmare. You can't tend to anything else or anyone else. You lack purpose— you can't imagine having a purpose.

I had been in Scotland a long time, and after this revelation, I was more than ready to go home. I missed my family. I wanted to get back to my wife and kids, see my father, my grandchild. I needed my family. We needed each other.

In my last communication with Jordan, via text message, we said that we loved each other. I had to hold on to that forever.

14

THIS IS NOT FAREWELL

"A man is probably less likely to be contradicted in lauding Prestwick than in singing the praises of any other course in Christendom."

—Bernard Darwin, *The Golf Courses of the British Isles*

I t was still early afternoon when I lost sight of Robbie's small white car in the distance over Machribeg Farm. Suddenly I didn't want to spend the rest of the day alone on Dunaverty Rock. The morning had been both grievous and uplifting. I felt emotionally drained. Hugh Sinclair, a friend in Campbeltown, had invited me to stop by his house for coffee. He lives on the hill above the west side of town, close to the Springbank Distillery. I had just two days before I could hop on my flight back home and see my family. Before I could say goodbye to Scotland, I had two more rounds to go: one of them an important return to the place where it all began for me and my dad. I had to see a few old friends: some of them were from my early visits with my dad.

My drive into town was slow and deliberate. The B842 ran close to the Coniegien River at several points. I stopped on the verge by a picturesque emerald field. The sound of the river flowing toward Brunerican Bay was only interrupted by the occasional bleating of sheep. There was plenty of time before I was due to be at Hugh's. I parked at the harbor in Campbeltown, in front of Taj Mahal Tandoori: an Indian restaurant my dad and I had visited several times in 1994. Brightly colored fishing boats sat quietly on the water, their work done for the day.

Around the corner, I passed by a small, hidden courtyard. On the black wrought-iron fence was a small sign for the Linda McCartney Memorial Garden. A beautifully sculpted bronze statue of Mrs. McCartney, holding a lamb, sat in the middle of the well-kept garden. The inscription read:

This Memorial Garden is dedicated to

The memory of Linda McCartney

Who did so much for her beloved Kintyre

I wondered to myself if Sir Paul had ever come here. I could not even imagine visiting the cemetery where Jordan is buried—it would be too soon and too much for me—but this felt different. It was a place of peace and reflection. For an American to be remembered this way, in such a remote part of Scotland, was an incredible honor. It might be greater than anything her husband ever achieved.

Before Jordan had become obsessed with golf, he was a child prodigy on guitar. He could play Beatles songs note for note on his bright red Gibson. It was amazing to watch him. A few weeks after his death, we found a "time capsule" he had made in fourth grade. Among other now heartbreaking things, he had listed, in careful handwriting, his favorite Beatles songs: "Ticket to Ride," "I Feel Fine," "Rain," "I'm Looking Through You," and "Eight Days a

Week." While sitting on a bench in this quiet place, I could see him playing for me in our den in Alabama. He always had the happiest smile when he played guitar. After yesterday at Dunaverty, I was coming to the realization that I could not suppress these types of memories.

On the way to Hugh's house, on a street curiously called The Roading, I passed by the Springbank Distillery. A side door on one of the old stone warehouses was propped open. Nobody was around, so I parked on the road and looked in the door. Golden-brown barley was spread out over a concrete floor among multi-colored steel support columns. Two men were raking the grain with long wooden poles. The level of craftsmanship and commitment it takes to make something the same way for 200 years was still valued here. In an expedient society where the world seems to start over every 24 hours, Springbank is a welcome outlier. I wasn't supposed to be there, so I watched for only a minute and left.

Hugh Sinclair (pronounced by most Scots as "Sink-ler") is a native of the tiny, former coal mining village of Drumlemble. It's located on the road between Campbeltown and Machrihanish. He was named for his grandfather, Hughie Sinclair, the longtime golf professional at the Machrihanish Ladies Golf Club. In 2019, Jake and I had played a wonderfully contested match at Machrihanish Dunes against Hugh and his best mate Hamish. After the golf, he picked us up at the Ardshiel Hotel for an evening meal at his home, prepared by his partner Sheena. Hamish and his wife were there. It was a memorable night of great food, conversation, and Jura whisky. We solved all the problems of golf.

A man of strong convictions, Hugh had resigned from his membership of over 50 years at Machrihanish Golf Club in 2019, for various personal reasons. "Sheena says it is none of my business now, but I still care about the place," he said, as we eased into our conversation. My host left the spacious, comfortable den to go prepare our coffee. Sheena was off to walk their dog, also named Hamish after Hugh's friend, and stopped to say hello. "It's so good to see you again, Jim. Hugh told me about your poor son. I am so sorry for your loss. I can't even imagine what your family is going through," she said with sadness in her voice. "I'm so glad you came to visit Hugh."

A few minutes later, Hugh returned with a cappuccino and a plate of biscuits. We discussed Dunaverty and the Dunes, but mostly talked about Machrihanish. "I don't understand why the club doesn't do more to promote its history. Old Tom is barely acknowledged," he lamented. The state of his game was also a topic. "I haven't been able to play much at all since you and Jake were here. My back has been a problem." He got up suddenly, exclaiming, "I want to show you something." He returned quickly with an ancient-looking hickory club, which he handed to me. It had a leather grip and was engraved on the back as a Super Mashie Niblick, roughly the equivalent to a modern-day 7 iron. In lovely script writing it was stamped, *H. Sinclair*, Machrihanish. Hugh is fiercely proud of his grandfather, who also worked in the Drumlemble mines. He then showed me a remarkable photo from the early 1900s of his grandfather and another young lad caddying at Machrihanish. As he walked me to my car, he said, "you have been in my thoughts for a while now, Jim. I hope being here has helped you. Please come back again."

On the way out of town, I stopped at my dad's favorite Indian restaurant and ordered a takeaway curry. There were no cars at Dunaverty Rock as I opened the cattle gate. Donnie MacLean must have completed his work for the day. I ate the curry on the back deck. The house was deathly silent, except for the sound of the wind. I took a pint of Tennent's down to the water. The sun was disappearing over the hills beyond the Keil Hotel. A cow walked slowly along the edge of the surf on Dunaverty Beach. "I wish you could see all of this, Jordan," I said to myself. The wind carried my words out over the Irish Sea.

The first ferry from Claonaig to Lochranza departs at 8:50. Ari Techner was meant to meet me there. On my way out the door, I left Donnie a thank-you note on the windowsill. On the narrow sandy track right behind the 4th green, I stopped the car. The dune overlooking the hidden dell below was covered in daisies and other small wildflowers. Unexpectedly, a line from an old R.E.M. song came into my mind: "The children look up, all they hear is sky-blue bells ringing." A bright yellow water hose was coiled on the short fringe—all the greens at Dunaverty are still watered by hand. From the top of the dune, I looked out over the links one final time. It looked like what I imagined heaven would be like.

Ari was waiting for me at the ferry slip. We were the second car in the queue. On the tailgate of the van in front of us, a young couple was preparing breakfast and coffee. My friend planned to leave his car at Claonaig and ride over with me to play Shiskine. Dougie Bell was alone in his shop when we arrived around 10:30. "Back for more already, Jim?," he asked. "Let's see, both of you are Dunaverty members so that's half price."

It was a beautiful, calm morning on the Kilbrannan Sound. Ari was amazed by his first visit to Shiskine, as I knew he would be. "Wow. Look at that. Unbelievable," he said, as we walked up the Crow's Nest and down the Shelf. Looking down the Shore Hole from the 7th tee, he said, "You could charge $250 in the US to play this, and people would line up to pay it."

"Thank God this isn't the US then," I replied quietly.

Back in the shop after the round, he asked Dougie Bell for a membership application.

At the ferry terminal, we said our goodbyes. Ari turned to me and said, "I hope to see you here again, Jim. You're welcome to stay with me in Campbeltown anytime." I promised to send him a copy of my book in a few weeks.

"You are living the life I dreamed for myself 30 years ago," I told him. It was back to the Corrie Hotel for my final night on Arran. On the way through Lochranza, I stopped to look for deer on the small, 11-hole golf course there.

Back at my same table in the corner of the Corrie Hotel bar, it was even busier than the week before. Time after time, Anne had to turn down a request for a table booking—either on the phone or for people who walked in. She had said, "I'm sorry, but we must take care of our residents first. I can do takeaway fish and chips for you."

In her short moments of quiet, we talked more about life on Arran.

"This island is so beautiful," I said after my second pint.

"Aye. I'm from here but you get used to it and take it for granted," she replied.

"Yes," I told her, "I've heard that a lot over the past month."

The 8:20 ferry from Brodick to Ardrossan was jammed with cars, vans, and lorries. It was good that I had booked it well ahead, on Robbie's advice. I would have never gotten on the ship otherwise. I stopped at Troon on the drive down to Prestwick, where I had a 1:30 tee time. The famous old links looked immaculate in the morning sun, with the most golfers I had seen in a month, many of them Americans. There was a sense of nervous anticipation as I sat on a bench behind the famous 18th green: the scene of so much Open drama. In a couple of hours, I was to be reunited with an old friend I had not seen in almost 20 years.

A handful of places remain—such as the Old Course and Prestwick—where full-time caddies are always available. Chris McBride has caddied on the Ayrshire coast since he was 13. Caddying is the only job he has ever had. He started out looping at Turnberry in the 1970s, working two days a week for 10 shillings a round—about the equivalent of 50 pence today. (For you Americans, that's less than a dollar.) Moving on to Royal Troon, he caddied during the week—eventually advancing to work the coveted weekend rounds. He learned the art of caddying through experience and observation. In 1987, he became a full-time caddie at Prestwick Golf Club, where he remains to this day, working 36 holes a day at the historic links whenever possible. "It took me a wee while to get in at Prestwick, but once you're in there, you're fine," he said now. There is nobody alive that understands the subtleties and mysteries of Prestwick better than Chris McBride.

Prestwick Golf Club is one of the special places in golf. At this ancient links, caddies are still viewed as an integral part of the game. Chris may be the last true embodiment of a Scottish tradition as old as the game itself. I had been fortunate to have him caddie "to" me at Prestwick on several occasions. After just the 3rd hole of our initial round together in the 1990s—we had met only 30 minutes earlier—he would simply offer a club and expect me to hit it. If I questioned his club selection, he would calmly explain his reasoning. He offered advice as he thought it was warranted: "You want to favor the right-hand side here." His counsel was given economically, but at just the right moment. He read the tricky Prestwick greens with unfathomable accuracy. As we progressed into that long-ago round, I remember thinking to myself, "this man is a genius."

Chris has seen everything in his 50 years of caddying. Even a partial list of golfers he has "been out with" around the links of Ayrshire is impressive: Gary Player, Ben Crenshaw, US and British Amateur champion Harvie Ward, Byron Nelson, Doug Sanders, Peter Jacobsen, and Payne Stewart are just a few. He once told Stewart, then the reigning US Open champion, that he could not reach the difficult par-four 10th from 226 yards with a 3 wood. With his caddie insisting that the only play was driver off the deck—Stewart declined and promptly struck his best 3 wood. "He was a fast player," Chris recalls, which is possibly the highest praise from an old Scottish caddie. The shot came up short of the green and rolled back another 30 yards. Walking up to play his third, the late American pro said with a laugh, "Chris, that is the best driver and 3 wood I've hit in 20 years. By God, you were right." Chris McBride is rarely wrong at Prestwick.

After caddying briefly for Dundee native and former Walker Cup player Steve Martin for a handful of events in the mid-1980s, Chris turned down an offer to work full time on the European Tour. "I just couldn't see living that way, sleeping in tents and train stations, and there was hardly any money in it back then," he says with a laugh. He had heard enough horror stories from older caddies to realize that the nomadic tour lifestyle was not for him. In the ensuing years, he has worked in The Open and Senior Open Championships at Royal Troon, Turnberry, and Royal St. Georges, as well as countless Open qualifiers and British Amateurs whenever they are held in Ayrshire.

In 1997, he caddied for the American professional Ken Duke in local qualifying and then The Open proper at Royal Troon. "He was playing lovely golf. He came second by a stroke in the qualifying at Glasgow Gailes. We were just very unlucky at Troon," said Chris. The afternoon draw for the opening round in the 1997 Open is legendary for the biblical weather that struck the Ayrshire coast. "It was a nightmare. An absolute nightmare. We were even par on the front nine and +9 on the back coming in. There wasn't a single green we could reach in regulation," he remembers.

Almost 25 years later, Chris has an amazing recall of that fateful round at Royal Troon: "it was driver-1 iron all the way home. We hit driver into 17, the par three, and came up 20 yards short." The 18th hole was essentially unplayable, with a 240-yard carry to reach the fairway. While waiting on the 18th tee, he saw a Troon member he knew and jokingly asked him how they were supposed to play the hole. "Hit it in the grandstand on the right and take a drop" was the response. "So I said to Ken, well you need to hit it in the grandstand and he says, 'well I can't do that!' and hits it straight down the middle and comes up short of the fairway. He had to hack out with a sand wedge." Jack Nicklaus, then age 57, shot even par on the back nine in the worst of the conditions that afternoon. Chris holds that round in the highest regard: "When I found out later that day what Jack had scored, I could not believe it. That is the greatest nine holes ever played in the history of golf."

The first time I parted ways with Chris was at the bar in the wonderful Prestwick Old Course Hotel, which I learned is now closed. He had invited me to join him and some other caddies for their daily post-round convocation. It was a lively discussion—centered around links golf and the then-US President Bill Clinton. As the evening wound down, he asked where we were off to play next. I said, somewhat proudly, "We are driving to Royal Dornoch in the morning." He looked at me as if I had just said I was flying to the moon: "Dornoch?!? The last time I went up there, the polar bears were picking up firewood." Over 20 years later, I can still hear the raucous laughter of a table full of Prestwick caddies.

In August 2000, I played four rounds at Prestwick, all with Chris

McBride on the bag. We had a wonderful two days with my dad and cousin Chris—Charles' flight had been canceled in Birmingham. With the generosity that Scots often display, Chris invited my cousin and I to meet him later at the Ayr train station for a night on the town. What followed was a night of food and drink that ranks as one of the favorite evenings of my entire life. After a lovely dinner—and several pints of Tennent's—we settled in at Chris's favorite pub for the requisite golf discussion. Knowing that I was something of a golf obsessive, he began to ask me random trivia questions on the history of the game, which I answered accurately time after time: "Who was Nicklaus paired with in the last round at St. Andrews in '78? Who finished third in the '77 Open at Turnberry?"

He finally said, "Aye, I've got one you can't answer, Jim. Name all 14 courses where the Open Championship has been held."

When I recited the 14th venue—Prince's at Sandwich, where Gene Sarazen won—he said with amazement, "well, I will be damned. You are the only person that has ever answered that one, except for one of the R&A guys I caddied for." Chris has a near encyclopedic knowledge of golf history, and I had managed to impress him. It was a moment that somehow more than made up for the earlier missed birdie putt for 79. We retired to his house for a final dram of whisky. Saying our goodbyes in the Ayr street in the wee hours of the morning—with our host refusing to take any money from us for the evening—he put us in a taxi back to the Prestwick Old Course Hotel. That was the last time I saw him for 20 years.

When you are young, it's easy to assume that things will always work out the way you expect them to. I thought I'd be back in Prestwick again soon, surely within a year or two at the most. Chris and I stayed in touch for a while. After the world economy collapsed in 2008, I was unable to visit Scotland again for many years. We lost touch as time went on. In 2019, I was finally back in Scotland with Jake. On our last day of golf, we played two rounds at Shiskine. I met a friend of Chris's on the course, by random chance, and we were suddenly back in touch.

My favorite Chris McBride story is one that I have told countless times over the years, but it never gets old. On my last round with him at Prestwick, it was a tough, windy afternoon. I had somehow birdied the 9th to get to even par for the round. We silently made the short walk to the 10th tee. The 470-yard, uphill par four—the same hole that got the best of three-time major winner Payne Stewart—was playing dead straight into a 25-mph wind. Chris wasn't saying much, which meant he was pleased with how we were playing. I felt that I owed him a good round.

Chris silently handed me the driver. I had the honor and was enjoying the moment, as anybody would. As I lined up the tee shot, I stopped and asked, "Chris, can I reach this green in two today?"

He replied, as grave as a judge, "Aye. Aye, Jim. You can indeed. Not a problem at all—as long as you hit three good shots."

Chris McBride was standing outside David Fleming's wonderful pro shop when I walked up. Despite our long years apart, there was no hesitation in his voice when he said, "Jim, my old friend! How are you getting on? I can always count on Americans to be on time, if nothing else." Always the caddie, he was worried about getting off the 1st tee as soon as possible. "We can go off now, Jim, the tee isn't busy," he said. I mentioned that a friend, Murray Allan, had asked to join, and we needed to give him a little more time. "Aye, I hope he gets here soon. It's wide open just now."

Murray made it, just in time, and we gathered on the 1st tee at Prestwick, the site of the first Open Championship. As if on cue, the train from Troon came roaring by. In my estimation, Chris had not changed one bit over the years. He was as philosophical as always.

"Is it a 4 or 5 iron, Chris?," I asked, as we stood close together by my golf bag.

"That is the question, is it not?," he replied, seriously.

On the 2nd tee, a favorite par three of mine, I told my caddie not to expect much out of my game. Then I vaguely mentioned that something very bad had happened recently in my family. He suddenly looked concerned and asked, "What's happened, Jim?" Not wanting to ruin the reunion with my friend and affect Murray's round, I said quietly that I'd tell him later. Chris eschews all forms of social media. "I'd rather just talk to people. I don't even have email," he said. He would not have learned of Jordan's death through anything I had posted online.

The round was a pure joy. My good shots made Chris smile, and he took my bad ones in stride. I hooked one way left on the difficult par-four 8th and he said, "No bother, Jim. We will get that one right enough. There are no lost balls. People just look in the wrong place." He found it, of course, in a decent lie. I hit one of my best shots of the day. "I knew there was still a golfer in there somewhere!" he exclaimed.

At the Alps, the legendary 17th hole played by everyone from Tommy Morris to Harry Vardon to Walter Hagen, I managed to hit my best drive of the day: a lovely high draw that found the middle of the wildly undulating fairway. The approach shot is totally blind. Chris seemed serious, suddenly. "I think it's just a wee 7, Jim, over the left-hand marker pole." I made the best swing of my entire month in Scotland. Within a second of the strike, Chris said quietly, "shot." If I live another 30 years, I will never get a greater compliment than that. "If that isn't close, I'm Margaret Thatcher," he said, striding up the hill proudly.

We crested that ancient sandhill, climbed by everyone of consequence in golf history, to see my ball about 10 feet from the pin. "That should be closer," said my caddie, almost defiantly. Chris studied the putt like it was for the Open Championship. In some ways, it was much more important. "If you hit just here, I think it will go," he said, pointing to a spot just outside the cup. I thought about Robbie's simple-but-needed advice to hit the middle of the putter face and made a smooth stroke. The ball rolled straight into the middle of the cup. "You just birdied the oldest hole in major championship golf!" said my old friend, excitedly.

He hugged me briefly. "Nobody can ever take that away from you, Jim."

Murray made a nice birdie on the 18th, and our day was made. We all shook hands in front of the old Prestwick clubhouse. Chris has never driven a car. "What do I need a car for? The train runs from Ayr to Prestwick," he had once told me. He got in my rental Toyota and we drove over to his pub in Ayr. It wasn't far from my room for the night—or from his house. We each ordered a Guinness: his drink of choice. I finally told him about Jordan's death. "Oh, my friend. This is so terrible. I don't even know what to say. How are you even able to walk around?," he asked. I shared all the horrible details. After yesterday, it was somehow a bit easier to tell him about everything. We caught up on all the long years apart. He had grandchildren now and they were clearly a great source of joy.

My flight home from the Glasgow airport was early the next morning. I had to cut the evening short. We walked out of the pub to say our goodbyes.

"This is not farewell, my friend. I will see you here again. I will keep you in my thoughts. God bless you," and he walked away toward his home. I watched him on the sidewalk for several seconds before losing him in the crowd.

It was time for me to go home, too. I couldn't wait.

I had parked close to my room for the night. I found a place to eat, then walked back to the beach to watch the sunset. It was a clear night. I realized that I could see Dunaverty in the far distance, past the southern tip of Arran. A young boy was throwing a tennis ball in the gentle surf to his dog. I smiled, and for the first time in what felt like a very long time, I did not cry.

EPILOGUE
LIGHT A CANDLE

> *"I have understood. And the certainty that there is nothing to understand should be my peace, my triumph."*
>
> —Umberto Eco, *Foucault's Pendulum*

> *"I will not say: do not weep; for not all tears are an evil."*
>
> —J.R.R. Tolkien, *The Return of the King*

The A9 winds down from Inverness and the Highlands through the Cairngorms. Tomorrow would be the one-year anniversary of Jordan's death, and I was back in Scotland. I had survived the *annus horribilis*, and in summer 2022, I was back at my spiritual home of Scotland. After playing the Boat of Garten Golf Club, I stopped at The Rod & Reel Pub to send Robbie a text message.

"I'm in Crianlarich. I'll be in Lochgilphead in 90 minutes or so."

"No bother, Jim. My dad is here. He wants to see you for a minute. We can go for fish and chips later if you like."

My legs were tight after walking "The Boat," a lovely James Braid design in the magical woodlands near the River Spey. I walked around the pub car park in the misty rain to try and loosen up. I was anxious to see my friend again.

As the terrible anniversary approached, I felt the urgent need to return to Scotland to see if there was something more to learn. After coming home to Alabama in September 2021, I had been able to adjust—as much as anyone can—to the reality of life without Jordan. My book was doing well, and architectural work had gotten busy again. I was able to play the occasional round of golf with my dad, Jonathan, and Jake. Our grandson Otis was a source of much joy for my wife and me. The revelation I experienced at Dunaverty had shown me the reason to continue. The grief was often crippling at times, but it was manageable. I had been able to carry on with life. Still, the thought of being at home on that day was inconceivable. I called Robbie, and we planned a short trip to Askernish and Isle of Harris in the Outer Hebrides. Our first stop would be the holy Isle of Iona, just off the southwest coast of the Isle of Mull.

We took the ferry from Oban to Craignure, then drove down through Mull. The narrow, winding road traversed rolling farmland and hidden glens beneath the mighty hills. From Fionnphort, a passenger ferry makes the short crossing over the narrow Sound of Iona to Baile Mor. No cars are allowed on the tiny 3.5-square-mile island. With golf bags over our shoulders, we walked down the slipway among the silent pilgrims making their way to Iona Abbey. An elderly Scottish gentleman smiled at us and asked incredulously, "There is a golf course on Iona?"

"We can only hope so," I replied.

It's a two-mile walk to the golf course from the ferry landing. Robbie had arranged for a friend at the abbey to pick us up in the works van. She seemed skeptical when she dropped us off at the edge of the tumbling machair. It was a cold, misty day and the wind was howling off the open Atlantic. As we stepped out on the sandy path, she said, "I'll pick you up here in two hours."

I had a surprise for my friend: an old British size Dunlop 65, still in the shiny, black and red wrapper. He unwrapped it on the first tee. Despite being over 50 years old, the ball was still a brilliant white, almost glowing in the gray mist. He struck it with an ancient-looking hickory driver, and it flew down the fairway, scattering a group of sheep as it landed.

The pristine, natural links was reminiscent of the Isle of Colonsay. Natural blow-out bunkers—the kind that modern day golf course designers could only hope to create—were scattered across the rocky machair. The turf was bouncy and resilient. On the 4th tee, perched high above the impossibly blue Atlantic, a small lamb chased its mother, then sprinted in front of me, just as I started my downswing. It was my best drive of the day, carrying a massive rocky hill and finding the fairway beyond.

After the round, we rode back to the abbey in silence. A large group of supplicants were gathered at the main entry to the cathedral. Ancient Celtic crosses stood vigil, seemingly impervious to the passage of time. The thick, heavy mist hung in the air like a shroud. We walked over to a small, gray stone chapel surrounded by bluebells, the burial place of the Kings of Scotland. It was just the two of us. We sat on an old wooden pew in silent respect.

Inside the soaring nave of the cathedral, a large gothic window provided a muted, dim light over the presbytery beyond. In a corner of the transept, I noticed a small altar of votive candles, next to a multi-colored, leaded glass window. I'm not sure how long I stood there before I felt a hand on my shoulder. Robbie said quietly, "you should light a candle for your wee boy, Jim. He was looking down on us today and smiling and laughing at us trying to get around Iona."

As the wick ignited, I felt tears run down my face. I said a silent prayer for those of us parents who continue.

AFTERWORD

BY WRIGHT THOMPSON

An afterword is a tricky, even silly, thing to try and write because what could there possibly be left to say that Jim Hartsell hasn't said so beautifully and perfectly. Anything else is stepping on the ending, as my editor used to tell me, but I do feel like I can somehow put words to what you are feeling, what we are all feeling, after getting to the end of this story.

When Jordan died, his father went to Scotland to try and find something there on these courses they'd loved. Jim writes about finding peace, but it's clear on every page that he was also looking for traces of his son in the ether, for some proof that Jordan's beau-tiful, powerful life force hadn't simply turned to dust and blown away. That his son was still with him somehow and that they could communicate. On the 3rd hole of one of those rounds, a hard dogleg, Jim saw something down by the green: a hulking red deer. The animal just lazily chewed grass and didn't seem startled by the men and their bags of sticks. Finally, the deer slipped into the woods.

Jim putted out first and walked along to the next tee. He crossed a bridge, and that's when he saw the deer again. Jim didn't move. Neither did the deer. Instead, the deer just stared at him. When Jim's playing partners arrived, the deer still didn't move. He remained behind, slowly vanishing into the Scottish mist, first a shadow, then just gone. Jim knew in his soul that Jordan was somehow communicating. It doesn't really matter what I believe or you believe, although for the record I firmly believe that the spirit world finds ways to speak to us.

That's the great gift of the book you just finished. One of its many gifts, to be more accurate, and the one that I appreciated the most. It is a story about a father and a son, about golf, about loss and grief and hope, but it is also a story about trying to fight the finality of death, trying to prove the reaper wrong, and letting love triumph in the end over grief.

I feel like Jordan is alive in these pages. I don't know whether that piece of him never died, or if his father brought him back to life, but his presence and energy vibrate off every page. I feel like my father was alive on these pages, and every other person lost to me, and to us, because this book is not just a roadmap for one human being's journey out of despair. No, it is a universal roadmap. It shows us *all* the way.

That's the magic of playing these old golf courses in Scotland, or a local muni where your memories rest with all the lost balls: when we walk these grassy fields, we walk with everyone who ever walked them with us. Most of the time those ghosts are invisible, vanished into the mist. But every once in a while, something happens that pulls them from the shadows and the darkening sky, and makes them as real as a deer standing by a green, not far from a thick woods and a small stream running to some peaty loch. This book does just that: it makes spirits come back to us and allows just one more slow walk in the grace of their company and love.

—Wright Thompson

ACKNOWLEDGMENTS

"Oh, and I remembered something you once told me
And I'll be damned if it did not come true.
Twenty thousand roads I went down, down, down
And they all led me straight back home to you."

—Gram Parsons, "The Return of the Grievous Angel"

I could not have made it through the last year and a half, and could not have written this book, without the help of so many people.

The person who deserves the most thanks is my friend Robbie Wilson. After Jordan's death, he welcomed me into his home in Lochgilphead without hesitation. I could never have spent a month in Scotland without his assistance. We have now traveled to such remote and beautiful places as Askernish, Iona, Isle of Harris, Colonsay, and Camusdarach Beach. We have seen things that people can only dream of seeing—like the Callanish Standing Stones on the Isle of Lewis. We have played golf at Shiskine with a great man like Willie Kelso. Robbie introduced me to Oban, now my favorite town, the Green Seafood Hut, and the music of Peat and Diesel. He has shown me the ancient, unbelievable history of Kilmartin Glen. He has introduced me to so many other great people, such as Harry MacLean and Jeff Butcher. The times we have spent together have been some of the best of my life. He has supported and encouraged my writing since we first met. There are no words sufficient for me to adequately thank him. A marauding cow will never trample me dead, Robbie.

Michael Bamberger has been very generous with his time. *To The Linksland* is the reason I went to Machrihanish for a week in 1994. His book was the reason my dad and I spent several days at Cruden Bay on that same trip. He is one of the main reasons that I continued to pursue my dream of being a writer. He has carried on the tradition of Bernard Darwin and Herbert Warren Wind, when many writers now only write for clicks on social media. In my opinion, he is the world's greatest living golf writer. Michael has read almost everything I have written. He has been complementary and encouraging while offering insightful critiques.

Stephen Proctor has provided thoughtful and brilliant conceptual suggestions throughout the entire process of the writing of this book. He is a great writer and, perhaps even more importantly, a brilliant reader. When I thought I was finished, he pushed me to dig even deeper into my emotions and keep going. The story is better because of him.

Wright Thompson is the best voice-over person in Open Championship history. He is also an eloquent writer. It is an honor that he offered to help me with this book.

I could not have written this book without the help of my editor, Jim Sitar. He understands my writing and knows exactly when to suggest that I need to go further. He made the hard, emotional work of writing this book enjoyable and healing. He is a brilliant editor.

A few selected portions of this story have appeared previously in *The Golfers Journal* and *The Links Diary*.

When *The Golfers Journal* approached me about writing a story on the tragedy of Jordan's death, I had already written my outline and a few chapters for this book. I was unsure about doing it, but I am glad that I did. Travis Hill and Tom Coyne offered minimal but crucial editing to a story that I wrote out in one sitting on a cold Saturday in Alabama. They were understanding and sympathetic to the extreme emotions involved in the telling of such a tragic tale—but could see the essence of hope that it might possibly offer to people. I cannot thank them enough for giving me the opportunity to contribute to the world's best literary golf journal.

Jamie Darling and Kenny Pallas of *The Links Diary* have become friends of mine. I have played golf with Jamie at his brilliant Lanark Golf Club and, of course, with Kenny at his beloved Panmure. They were the first publication to give me a chance as a writer and I will never forget that. Their love of Scotland and Scottish golf is reflected in every issue of *The Links Diary*. I had sent versions of my story on Chris McBride, "The Last Caddie," to several publications—generally not even receiving as much as a polite rejection notice. As soon as Jamie read it, he said, "This is one of the best things I've ever read." It is an honor to continue to write for them and their lovely Scottish golf journal.

Others that I must thank include: the great Chris McBride, Tom Morton, Harry MacLean, Jeff Butcher, Greg McCrae, Hamish Bannantyne, Tom Shaw, Joshua Ralston, Alasdair MacDougall, Donnie MacLean, Shannon Wilson, Gregor Cameron, Hugh Sinclair, Ari Techner, Rob Collins, John Allen, Kevin Moore, Todd Schuster, Phil Landes, Tony Dear, Lorne Rubenstein, Ru McDonald, Malcolm Duck, Kevin Van Valkenburg, Robbie Fields, Coach Chad Gladden, Chris Hartsell, Charles Hartsell, Jammy Erwin, Robin and Gabe Fuller, Lam Tong, Lynn Layton, and Sir Davy Wilson of Lochgilphead.

Only my family truly understands the crushing grief of losing Jordan. The world moves on, as it must, but we do not have that luxury. My sons, Jonathan and Jake, are good people. They have dealt with the death of their precious little brother as courageously as possible. Whenever I look at photos of the three of them together, from when Jordan was a little boy, they are holding onto him for dear life. The years that we all lived together in this house were the best years of my life. I hope we can play golf together for many more years. I hope we can stand on Dunaverty Beach together and remember their brother. My wife Jaymaine has suffered greatly. She was extremely close to Jordan. I am thankful that she has been understanding of the way that I have tried to deal with this tragedy. My dad, Lee Hartsell, loved his grandson as only a grandfather can. He helped teach him how to play golf. He rode with us to countless tournaments, always studying the scoreboard after every round—trying to figure out exactly how Jordan was going to win. He has been a great dad. Our many trips together to Scotland and Ireland started me on the long journey that led to writing this book.

APPENDIX:

My 100 Favorite Holes in Scotland

Authors note: My criteria are a mixture of fun, natural beauty, strategy, quirkiness, and other intangible factors that are not explainable. This is not intended to be a list of the greatest championship holes in the country. I have played these courses at least once since 1994.

1. 4th at Dunaverty – Par 3, 177 yards
2. 8th at Cruden Bay – Par 4, 250 yards
3. 7th at Machrihanish – Par 4, 429 yards
4. 6th at Shiskine – Par 4, 274 yards
5. 5th at Golspie – Par 4, 288 yards
6. 11th at Askernish – Par 3, 197 yards
7. 12th at Hopeman – Par 3, 150 yards
8. 10th at Elie – Par 4, 288 yards
9. 11th at Dunaverty – Par 4, 266 yards
10. 17th at Prestwick – Par 4, 394 yards
11. 8th at Gairloch – Par 5, 526 yards
12. 14th at North Berwick – Par 4, 376 yards
13. 18th at The Old Course – Par 4, 354 yards
14. 8th at Panmure – Par 4, 360 yards
15. 1st at Brora – Par 4, 297 yards
16. 2nd at Corrie – Par 3, 199 yards
17. 3rd at Machrihanish – Par 4, 373 yards
18. 8th at Durness – Par 4, 377 yards

19. 4th at Isle of Harris – Par 3, 145 yards
20. 7th at Cullen – Par 3, 224 yards
21. 6th at Anstruther – Par 3, 128 Yards
22. 2nd at Traigh – Par 5, 452 yards
23. 3rd at Shiskine – Par 3, 127 yards
24. 1st at Isle of Skye – Par 4, 307 yards
25. 6th at Royal Dornoch – Par 3, 164 yards
26. 3rd at Fraserburgh – Par 4, 331 yards
27. 17th at The Old Course – Par 4, 461 yards
28. 16th at Golspie – Par 3, 175 yards
29. 12th at Isle of Colonsay – Par 4, 324 yards
30. 16th at Prestwick – Par 4, 290 yards
31. 2nd at Carradale – Par 4, 341 yards
32. 10th at Royal Dornoch – Par 3, 150 yards
33. 14th at Crail – Par 3, 147 yards
34. 2nd at Bute – Par 4, 324 yards
35. 7th at Gullane No. 1 – Par 4, 398 yards
36. 5th at Prestwick – Par 3, 206 yards
37. 8th at Royal Troon – Par 3, 126 yards
38. 16th at Turnberry – Par 4, 409 yards
39. 6th at Royal Aberdeen – Par 5, 487 yards
40. 5th at Fortrose & Rosemarkie – Par 3, 133 yards
41. 4th at Helmsdale – Par 4, 301 yards
42. 4th at Cruden Bay – Par 3, 196 yards
43. 4th at Iona – Par 4, 341 yards
44. 17th at Fortrose & Rosemarkie – Par 4, 383 yards
45. 16th at Wick – Par 4, 394 yards
46. 3rd at Cruden Bay – Par 4, 268 yards
47. 11th at Tain – Par 4, 380 yards
48. 4th at Rosehearty – Par 4, 293 yards
49. 2nd at Isle of Harris – Par 4, 299 yards
50. 5th at Montrose – Par 4, 292 yards
51. 9th at Dunbar – Par 5, 507 yards
52. 13th at Peterhead – Par 4, 423 yards
53. 15th at Boat of Garten – Par 4, 305 yards

54. 9th at Dunaverty – Par 4, 253 yards
55. 8th at Nairn – Par 4, 359 yards
56. 1st at Machrie Bay – Par 4, 303 yards
57. 8th at Portmahomack (Tarbat) – Par 4, 297 yards
58. 3rd at Comrie – Par 3, 157 yards
59. 9th at Reay – Par 3, 176 yards
60. 9th at The Old Course – Par 4, 307 yards
61. 16th at Askernish – Par 4, 363 yards
62. 11th at Gullane No. 1 – Par 4, 471 yards
63. 4th at Killin – Par 4, 370 yards
64. 5th at Muirfield – Par 5, 559 yards
65. 5th at Machrihanish Dunes – Par 3, 130 yards
66. 8th at Rothesay – Par 3, 183 yards
67. 13th at The Glen – Par 3, 148 yards
68. 7th at Gairloch – Par 3, 87 yards
69. 3rd at Elie – Par 3, 214 yards
70. 8th at Isle of Skye – Par 4, 294 yards
71. 12th at Panmure – Par 4, 361 yards
72. 13th at Cullen – Par 3, 152 yards
73. 6th at Carradale – Par 4, 306 yards
74. 9th at Western Gailes – Par 4, 336 yards
75. 6th at Machrihanish – Par 4, 311 yards
76. 15th at Askernish – Par 4, 326 yards
77. 13th at Gleneagles (King's) – Par 4, 448 yards
78. 7th at Golspie – Par 4, 285 yards
79. 9th at Covesea – Par 3, 104 yards
80. 7th at Shiskine – Par 3, 173 yards
81. 17th at Dunaverty – Par 4, 412 yards
82. 13th at Brora – Par 3, 125 yards
83. 9th at Anstruther – Par 3, 238 yards
84. 5th at Tarbert – Par 4, 332 yards
85. 14th at Carnoustie – Par 5, 488 yards
86. 7th at Fraserburgh – Par 3, 165 yards
87. 6th at Isle of Colonsay – Par 4, 301 yards
88. 5th at Durness – Par 4, 300 yards

89. 3rd at Bute – Par 3, 162 yards
90. 3rd at Corrie – Par 4, 248 yards
91. 6th at Portmahomack (Tarbat) – Par 4, 353 yards
92. 18th at North Berwick – Par 4, 274 yards
93. 8th at Traigh – Par 4, 367 yards
94. 6th at Dunaverty – Par 3, 245 yards
95. 16th at Reay – Par 4, 314 yards
96. 6th at Isle of Seil – Par 4, 270 yards
97. 1st at Stonehaven – Par 4, 305 yards
98. 14th at Loch Lomond – Par 4, 345 yards
99. 12th at Lanark – Par 4, 355 yards
100. 1st at Lochcarron – Par 3, 215 yards

BIBLIOGRAPHY

"You only have to read the lines
Of scribbly black and everything shines"
—Syd Barrett, Pink Floyd, "Matilda Mother"

Atkinson, Tom. *The Lonely Lands: A Guidebook to Argyll* (Barr, Scotland, 1985).

Baillie, Hugh. *Golf at the Back of Beyond: Brora Golf Club, 1891-2000* (Brora, Scotland, 2008).

Bamberger, Michael. *To The Linksland: A Golfing Adventure* (New York, 1992).

Bannantyne, Colin C. *The Shiskine Golf & Tennis Club: A History, 1896-1996* (Blackwaterfoot, Scotland, 1996).

Barrett, Syd. *The Lyrics of Syd Barrett* (London, 2021).

Caldwell, David H. *Islay, Jura and Colonsay: A Historical Guide* (Edinburgh, 2001).

Campbell, Thorbjorn. *Arran: A History* (Edinburgh ,2007).

Corcoran, Michael. *Duel in the Sun* (New York, 2002).

Darwin, Bernard. *British Golf* (London, 1946).

Darwin, Bernard. *James Braid* (London, 1952).

Darwin, Bernard. *The Darwin Sketchbook* (USA, 1991).

Darwin, Bernard. *The Golf Courses of the British Isles* (London, 1910).

Dickinson, Patric. *A Round of Golf Courses* (London, 1951).

Dodson, James. *Final Rounds: A Father, A Son, The Golf Journey of a Lifetime* (New York, 1996).

Drummond, Maldwin. *West Highland Shores* (London, 1990).

Eco, Umberto. *Foucault's Pendulum* (Milan, 1988).

Fallon, Jim. *Tarbat Golf Club (Portmahomack): The First 100 Years* (Portmahomack, 2009).

Greig, Andrew. *Preferred Lies: A Journey to the Heart of Scottish Golf* (London, 2006).

Haultain, Arnold. *The Mystery of Golf* (Boston, 1908).

Huber, Jim, *Four Days In July: Tom Watson, The 2009 Open Championship, And a Tournament for the Ages* (New York, 2011).

Hutchinson, Horace. *British Golf Links* (London, 1897).

Johnson, Samuel. *A Journey to the Western Islands of Scotland* (London, 1775).

Kerr, John. *The Golf Book of East Lothian* (Edinburgh, 1896).

Lang, Andrew. *A Short History of Scotland* (Edinburgh, 1911).

MacKenzie, Alister. *The Spirit of St. Andrews* (Chelsea, MI, 1995).

MacMillan, Nigel S.C. *The Campbeltown & Machrihanish Light Railway* (Newton Abbot, England, 1970).

MacVicar, Angus. *Dunaverty Golf Club: The First Hundred Years* (Campbeltown, Scotland, 1989).

MacVicar, Angus. *Golf In My Gallowses* (London, 1983).

MacVicar, Angus. *Heather In My Ears* (London, 1974).

Martin, Angus. *Kintyre: The Hidden Past* (Kilkerran, Scotland, 1984).

McCarthy, Cormac. *Blood Meridian: Or the Evening Redness in the West* (New York, 1985)

McDiarmid, D.J. *100 Years of Golf at Machrihanish* (Campbeltown, Scotland, 1976).

McKinlay, S.L. *Scottish Golf and Golfers: A Collection of Weekly Columns from the Glasgow Herald, 1956-1980* (Stamford, CT, 1992).

McPhee, John. *The Crofter and the Laird* (New York, 1970).

Moreton, John F. and Ian Cumming. *James Braid and his Four Hundred Golf Courses* (Worcestershire, 2013).

Morton, Tom. *Hell's Golfer: A Good Walk Spoiled* (Edinburgh, 1994).

Murphy, Michael. *Golf In The Kingdom* (New York, 1972).

Nalder, Ian. *Scotland's Golf in the Days of Steam: A Selective History of the Impact of the Railways on Golf* (Dalkeith, Scotland, 2000).

Pearson, Joanl. *Kilmartin: The Stones of History* (Gartocharn, Scotland, date unknown).

Proctor, Stephen. *Monarch of the Green: Young Tom Morris, Pioneer of Modern Golf* (Edinburgh, 2019).

Ritchie, Graham and Mary Harman. *Argyll and the Western Isles* (Edinburgh, 1985).

Rubenstein, Lorne. *A Season in Dornoch: Golf and Life in the Scottish Highlands* (New York, 2003).

Steel, Donald. *Classic Golf Links of England, Scotland, Wales, and Ireland* (Gretna, LA, 1992).

Updike, John. *Golf Dreams: Writings on Golf* (New York, 1996).

Ward-Thomas, Pat. *The Long Green Fairway* (London, 1966).

Webb, Sharon. *In the Footsteps of Kings: A Guide to Walks in and Around Kilmartin Glen* (Kilmartin, Scotland, 2012).

Wilson III, D.M. and H.R.J. Grant. *Machrihanish: Machaire Shanais, Golf 1880s-1920s* (Worcestershire, 2018).

Wind, Herbert Warren. *Following Through: Herbert Warren Wind On Golf* (New York, 1985).

Withall, Mary. *Easdale, Belnahua, Luing & Seil: The Islands that Roofed the World* (Glasgow, 2001).

ABOUT THE AUTHOR

Jim Hartsell is a native and lifelong resident of Alabama.
A registered architect, he has worked on the design of projects for
the University of Alabama, Jacksonville State University, University
of Georgia and University of Florida. Scottish golf and golf writing
are his true passions, having made many trips to Scotland to study
the lesser-known courses. He is the author of *The Secret Home of
Golf: The Authorized History of King-Collins Golf and the Creation of
Sweetens Cove* (2021). He has written extensively on golf in Scotland
for *The Links Diary*, NoLayingUp.com and is a contributor to *The
Golfers Journal* and *Today's Golfer*.

Made in the USA
Las Vegas, NV
04 December 2024

de2b779a-60cd-43b3-9a2b-63808cd419abR01